AF248783

CONFESSIONS
OF TWO BROTHERS

CONFESSIONS OF TWO BROTHERS

John Cowper Powys
Llewelyn Powys

With an introduction by Malcolm Elwin

Sinclair Browne: London

Confessions of two Brothers first published New York, 1916.
This edition first published 1982 in the United Kingdom by
Sinclair Browne Ltd, 10 Archway Close, London N19 3TD

Introduction © Eve Elwin 1982
Confessions by John Cowper Powys © Francis Powys 1982
Confessions by Llewelyn Powys © Eve Elwin 1982

British Library Cataloguing in Publication Data:
Powys, John Cowper
   Confessions of two brothers.
   1. Powys, John Cowper 2. Powys, Llewelyn
   3. Authors, English—20th century—Biography
   I. Title II. Powys, Llewelyn
   823'.912   PR6031.0867

   ISBN 0–86300–004–5
   ISBN 0–86300–005–3 Pbk

Printed in Great Britain by
Redwood Burn Limited, Trowbridge, Wiltshire
and bound by Pegasus Bookbinding, Melksham, Wiltshire

Publisher's note

The text of *Confessions of two Brothers* has
been reproduced lithographically from the
New York edition of 1916. It contains a
number of printer's errors which it was not
practicable to correct, most notably the
persistent mis-spelling of Llewelyn's name.

Acknowledgements
Acknowledgement is made to Laurence
Pollinger Ltd for permission to quote from
Welsh Ambassadors by 'Louis Marlow' and
from *The Secret Springs* by Claude Bragdon.

Introduction

Confessions of Two Brothers is surely a unique book. This is the first English edition, yet it was published in New York as long as sixty six years ago and its authors were two Englishmen living on opposite sides of the world, the one a lecturer in the United States, the other (under strong protest) a sheep farmer in East Africa. Though they were to become famous as two of the three celebrated Powys brothers and between them authors of about eighty books, both were then virtually unknown writers; the younger had published some magazine stories, the elder was author of two slim volumes of verse, a few pamphlets, a book of essays, and a first novel called *Wood and Stone*, which was dismissed by critics as an imitation of Thomas Hardy and did not find a publisher in England (copies are now collectors' items at fantastic prices).

Have two brothers ever before or since collaborated in a volume of autobiography so early in their literary careers? Truly they were not young. In February 1916, when *Confessions of Two Brothers* was published by the Manas Press of Rochester, New York, John Cowper Powys was in his forty-fourth year, his brother

INTRODUCTION

Llewelyn in his thirty-second. With hindsight the modern reader of this book may well think it obvious that these two brothers were likely to become famous writers. Each shows himself to be a remarkable man, each with a strikingly individual style of self-expression, each with a habit of thought in advance of their own time— indeed, as events have proved, their thought is still in advance of our time to-day, and they write with a frankness that is still unfashionable in a world of self-deceivers.

How then did it happen that no English publisher could be found for such a book on its first appearance in America? Of course 1916 was in the middle of what used to be called 'The Great War' and has been called 'The First World War' since politicians proved criminally stupid enough to involve everybody in a second such disaster. In wartime there is always a paper shortage because governments commandeer so much of the supply for coupons, ration books, identity papers, permits, forms to be filled in—all the paraphernalia of slavery that is immediately introduced when political propaganda has precipitated nations into a state of funk.

Though Barabbas was certainly a publisher, John Cowper Powys may have exaggerated a little when writing to his brother Llewelyn in 1939 that 'Publishers are all cheats, rogues and villains'. But he was right enough when he wrote,

INTRODUCTION

'nor are Publishers critics of literature as a rule'. Some publishers have had the gumption to employ professional men of letters to advise them: for thirty years George Meredith was reader to Chapman & Hall; on setting up in business, Jonathan Cape engaged Edward Garnett, who advised him to publish successively both Llewelyn and John Cowper; I myself kept the wolf off the threshold by twenty one years as literary adviser to Macdonalds, who published all John Cowper's books from *Porius* till his death.

Before this modern age, when big commercial combines absorb publishing houses to run them deliberately at a loss for taxation purposes, a few able eccentrics sometimes became publishers. There were Martin Secker, who published Compton Mackenzie and D.H. Lawrence, and Charles Prentice, who made for Chatto & Windus a distinguished list that included T.F. Powys, Sylvia Townsend Warner, Aldous Huxley, and that tippling old rascal, Norman Douglas. Such an eccentric briefly established the Manas Press, 'a private, non-profitmaking venture,' named from a Sanskrit word meaning Thought or Mind.

He was Claude Bragdon, born in the same year as H.G. Wells—an architect by profession, who turned writer, theatrical designer, occultist and philosopher, besides being a publisher. In his autobiography, *The Secret Springs* (1939), he relates how he met John Cowper Powys when he came to Rochester to lecture. In Chapter IX of these *Confessions* Powys declares that his main object as a lecturer was 'to instill a little imagination into the public's mind', but he admits also that he loved to expatiate on the influence wrought upon him by books and their writers as 'the atmosphere of one's life-drama'. He told Bragdon that his lecturing 'enabled him to rid himself of certain hates and loathings which, undischarged, would poison him, mentally and physically'.

Bragdon remembered how 'people flocked to witness his fireworks, even when they got singed by them'. Women abounded in his audiences, for he was a man of striking good looks, six feet tall, with aquiline features, thick curling dark hair, and eyes expressively reflecting every changing mood—in his prime he must have suited the dress of a Red Indian chief. Bragdon thought 'he liked to jog' his audiences 'out of their complacencies— to make them squirm—even while he awakened in them new perceptions'. Once he horrified his agent as well as the women in his audience by beginning, 'Ladies, you know we all like to have our sexual life go on pleasantly'. This was before 1914, and some women's organisation 'vowed never to have him speak to them again—but they did have him.'

Wearing his flowing Cambridge gown and pacing up and down the platform, he seemed to

Bragdon 'like a big black spider spinning a web of words with which to ensnare the minds of the unwary', or in another mood 'a black-robed priest ... communicating the eternal truth of things'. Others have testified to his fascination as a lecturer: Maurice Browne—mentioned in Chapter XI of these *Confessions* as 'that inspired Idealist', the manager of the Little Theatre at Chicago, later to become producer of R.C. Sheriff's famous success, *Journey's End*—describes him in *Too Late to Lament* (1955) as 'incomparably the finest public speaker' he ever heard, not excepting Winston Churchill in the war years: 'he identified himself with his subject, almost invariably a literary subject... The man was a great actor'. When Cecil Roberts—as he relates in *The Bright Twenties* (1970)—first lectured in the States as a young man he had the same lecture manager, who said of Powys, 'He looks like a necromancer and you wonder what he's going to conjure up, what voodoo he has up his wide sleeve. I've never met such a flood of intellect'.

Bragdon relates how the conductor Barnhart was absorbed in listening to Powys lecture on Dostoievsky and exclaimed at the end, 'That man is a wonderful person; but he's all tangled up in his *mind*'. Tangled he was, because he had read so much and absorbed so much in every daily experience of a much-travelled life. 'The important thing with any writer is his own soul', he once wrote; 'what he's got in his own head, in his own nerves, and in his own character and blood and temperament'. These early *Confessions* supply a key to the great writer that John Cowper became. Here he is beginning to resolve the tangle within himself; he is learning to expound the labyrinthine mysteries of what he called his 'life-illusion'. All the great novels that he was later to write—especially those which G. Wilson Knight has called 'the famous narratives'— result from 'the art of escaping from myself', which, as he tells here, he learned 'by long practice'; he uses nature, as the poet Redwood Anderson said, 'as the manifold expression of his single personality, so that, far from him remaining out of the picture, every face on the canvas, be it never so crowded and they never so distinct, is yet an aspect of a multitudinous and all-embracing self-portrait'.

At the start of these *Confessions* John Cowper warns his reader that 'he must follow me suspiciously, guardedly, furtively', always 'on the lookout for indirect betrayals and unmaskings'. By contrast there is never any mistaking his brother Llewelyn's meaning; he learned early to write with lucidity and power because he was always aware that he might have little time to spare, for though he lived to be fifty five, his last thirty years were haunted by the spectre of pulmonary tuberculosis. Even as he lay ill, he distilled the essence of fresh sensations and wrote when he could, with his elbow held rigid lest its movement might start a haemorrhage in his chest. When he knew that he was dying, he wrote, as his 'last word' to the world he was leaving, 'Love life! Love every moment of life that you experience *without pain*'.

As will be seen when their abundant correspondence is published, there was a bond between John Cowper and Llewelyn Powys beyond mere brotherliness. Each was a contrast with the other, yet the other's essential complement. This was the more curious from there being a gap of a dozen years between their ages. John Cowper, born on 8 October 1872, was the eldest of the eleven children born to the Rev. Charles Francis Powys by his wife, Mary Cowper Johnson. Three brothers and three sisters intervened between him and Llewelyn, born on 13 August 1884. Both were educated at Sherborne School and Corpus Christi College, Cambridge. At school John's eccentricities rendered him a ready victim for ragging till he became a prefect and established authority by using his gift of rhetoric in an impassioned speech, in which he derided the stupidity of his own eccentricities and the greater stupidity of those who mocked them, ending by shaking hands with his principal persecutors. At the same school Llewelyn was popular, an apparently normal boy who played cricket and football with gusto.

Yet it was at Sherborne, as he tells in these *Confessions*, that 'under the shadow of the grey abbey I gradually awakened to the continuous poetry of life set as it was against so immemorial and romantic a background'. Here too he confesses that he 'came to learn for the first time of the passionate and tremulous emotions which lie at the back and root of all life'. He says that he 'began to take the spell of the school chapel very lightly', and 'it was at this time that my brother, J.C.P., began giving me books'. It was when he found himself in a 'whirlpool of doubts' about the Christian faith that he appealed to his eldest brother after the schoolmasters had failed to help him—after they had told him that it was wrong to abandon himself to poetic and sensual emotion and that he would never be able to lead men if he was incompetent to command himself. John not only lent him books, but wrote him wise letters that have been preserved and will be published one day (when they find a publisher who knows his business). This was the beginning of the bond between the brothers.

At Cambridge Llewelyn made a lifelong friendship with Louis Wilkinson, who, as Louis Marlow, was to write *Welsh Ambassadors* (1936, new ed. 1971), a study of his friendship with the

Powys brothers. 'His smile alone, with its broad sudden light', wrote Wilkinson, was 'enough to win the stoniest heart... With his crisp curly bright hair and fair complexion, he had a sunlike look; he was dazzlingly bright. He had light eyes, eager and easily troubled, a rich unguarded mouth, a child's soft mouth greedy of pleasure and sometimes sulky. His body was hard and slight, with a hint of frailness, though no one would then have anticipated that he was so soon to be consumptive. His unusually large head seemed larger than it was because of its stiff woolly growth of light gold curls'.

Having enjoyed his fun at Cambridge, he felt he had wasted his time, especially after he had ploughed his history tripos and taken only a pass degree. Briefly but graphically he tells of his unhappy attempts to be a schoolmaster and a private tutor. The schools he describes were St Peter's Court, Broadstairs, and Bromsgrove in Worcestershire. But even after all these years the name of the family at Calne had better be suppressed, for they were rich people with the power to oppress that accompanies too much money.

'It was now', he says in beginning Chapter III of these *Confessions*, 'that I fell more completely than ever under the influence of my brother J.C.P.'. But in fact it was in the previous year that John had begun to fall under the influence of his much younger brother. In 1907 John was seriously ill and suffered his first operation for duodenal ulcer. Obviously his tendency to ulcers was aggravated by the emotional exertion of his lecturing, and Llewelyn urged him to earn his living by writing instead of by lecturing. He wrote stories which have never been published and took three years over writing a study of Keats, which was rejected as too outspoken for the current taste by the same publisher as later withdrew Lawrence's *Rainbow* from publication.

As Llewelyn was to write in *Damnable Opinions* and *Glory of Life*, we all live in traps, often in traps of our own making. In 1896 John had married a sister of his Cambridge friend T.H. Lyon (the T.H.L. mentioned in the last chapter of his *Confessions*), the marriage proved incompatible, and after the birth of a son in 1902 John had to live on a pittance himself while providing for the education of his son and for his wife's comforts as a county lady in an admirable house in Sussex. Llewelyn was infuriated that his eldest brother should be expending his gifts on exhausting lecture tours, but it was not for more than another twenty years that John—after his son had graduated at Cambridge and started to make his own living—was able to leave lecturing and settle to the writing of those great novels and philosophical books of which *Wolf Solent* and *The Meaning of Culture* were the first.

In 1905 John had discovered that the best

INTRODUCTION

market for university extension lecturing was in America, and every year till after the outbreak of war in 1914 he spent the winter months as an itinerant lecturer in the United States and the summers in England. To escape from schoolmastering Llewelyn was persuaded to join his brother in lecturing, and while John coached him in the craft, they enjoyed together those talks and excursions to which Llewelyn here briefly refers and which John recalled in relating the story of Rook and Lexie Ashover in his fourth novel, *Ducdame*. Together the brothers sailed to America in December 1908; only a few months after his return in the spring of 1909, Llewelyn, one morning coughed up blood and remembered the words of Keats: 'I know the colour of that blood; that blood is arterial blood; it is my death warrant; I must die!'

Before leaving for another lecture tour in America, John accompanied Llewelyn to the sanatorium in Switzerland where he remained for sixteen months and wrote most days the 'Consumptive's Diary' from which he gives brief extracts in these *Confessions*—(the diary is given more fully in my *Life of Llewelyn Powys*). He returned, partially cured and fetched home by John, at the end of April 1911 in time to enjoy in Somerset the brilliant summer described in that beautiful book, *Skin for Skin*.

Perhaps because he already had it in mind that

he would one day write *Skin for Skin*, Llewelyn telescopes events at this stage of his *Confessions*. In January 1912 he again visited Switzerland and prejudiced his recovery by a reckless expedition across the mountains from Arosa to Davos, as described in *Skin for Skin*. On his return in the spring of 1912 he was submerged in that 'wave of apathy' from which he was rescued by visiting Venice with his brother John, Louis Wilkinson, and the first of ,Louis's four wives, Frances Gregg, a girl from Philadelphia with whom all three were in love.

This love for their friend's wife went deeper with John than with Llewelyn, for John remained devoted to her for many years and was still her friend after her marriage had ended by divorce and he himself had found happiness with the woman who shared the last forty years of his life. But the romantic urge conspired with his illness to consolidate for Llewelyn the 'poetic faith' he expounded in *Impassioned Clay*, *Glory of Life*, and *Damnable Opinions*. He says himself. 'My illness had sharpened my wits', and this was emphasised by Louis Wilkinson in 1935; 'His consumption is important; for, heightening his sense of life's value, the disease, from its onset to the present year, has quickened and intensified all his perceptions'. The photograph of Llewelyn at fifty (reproduced as frontispiece to his *Life*) reflects his character: fringed by the golden hair and beard then rapidly silvering, his face and brow are lined by suffering and thought, but the shrewd and humorous eyes still reveal, as he lay on his bed of sickness, all 'his awareness, his vitality, his zest', which had fascinated Louis Wilkinson since he first knew him as a Cambridge undergraduate.

He was then two years at Montacute in Somerset from the autumn of 1912 till he left England for Africa in August 1914, a few weeks after war was declared. 'It was in Africa', he wrote in his last book, *Love and Death*, 'that I consolidated my philosophy'. For five years, while from Europe came monotonous bulletins of misery and slaughter unparalleled in human history, he watched the merciless forces of Nature motivelessly at play against a background of primitive majesty. Recalling his experiences, he wrote in *Black Laughter* a classic description of life in the tropics, and epitomised its moral lesson in the first chapter of *Damnable Opinions*. In England, 'with the holly tree standing outside the kitchen window year after year, with the baker bringing bread to the back-door day after day', the system of civilisation had so created a sense of security that it was 'easy to acquiesce in the illusion of man's regulated life'. But 'in Africa the compromises of human society are shown to be artificial ... It is no longer possible to be fooled'.

While Llewelyn was forming his philosophy as a sheep-farmer on the edge of the African jungle, John found himself forced by the war into writing for a living. Though America came even later into the first war than into the second, news from Europe distracted the people from attempting to improve their minds by attending lectures. His lecture agent turned publisher, and as early as October 1914 John wrote *The War and Culture*, a reply to the propaganda of a German-American professor named Münsterberg. A book of essays on some of his favourite writers, *Visions and Revisions*, appeared in February 1915, and his first novel, *Wood and Stone*, in the following November.

On 20 February 1915 John wrote to Llewelyn his idea of a book to be called *Confessions by the Six Brothers Powys*. 'Why shouldn't the Powys Brothers compose such a book as has never in the History of the World ever been written?' he asked. 'I love the idea of all of us going down to posterity together, even as we have lived!' But the impulse to write was less in three of the brothers; the youngest was already in the army, another (A.R. Powys, the architect) was soon to be a prisoner of war in Germany. Besides Llewelyn, only Theodore (T.F. Powys) sent a contribution to John in New York; for his *Soliloquy of a Hermit* John secured publication by his agent, Arnold Shaw. It was Llewelyn's contribution that impressed Claude Bragdon, who thought it 'brilliantly done, with touches of mordant humour deliberately calculated to shock the puritanical, such as: "Some women are made only for embraces, and should never be permitted out of their beds"', and 'John supplemented it with one of those long essays in introspection at which he was a past master'.

This book is a springboard from which to take off on a voyage of exploration into the works of two great writers. Both were prolific; considering their late start as writers, their output was immense. Llewelyn remained in Africa till 1919, when his youngest brother returned from war service to take over the farm; in 1920 he joined John in the United States and made his mark as a writer with stories and sketches about Africa in the *New York Evening Post*. He tells of his life in America in *The Verdict of Bridlegoose*. He married Alyse Gregory in 1924 and returned the following year to live in Dorset. Twice again he visited America, and also made a journey to Palestine—described in *A Pagan's Pilgrimage*—for the background of his enthralling distillation of the Bible in *The Cradle of God*. Disease laid him low in 1933, but living in an open shelter on the Dorset downs, he continued to write. The last three years of his life, before his death on 2 December 1939, were spend in Switzerland; *Love and Death*, the last book published during his lifetime, was said to be an imaginary romance, but was actually based on a love affair that deepened his poetic faith, as appears in *So Wild a Thing: Letters to Gamel Woolsey*.

His brother John had published *Wolf Solent*, the first of his most important novels, before his trouble with stomach ulcers drove him from lecturing to live by writing. During four years at Hillsdale in New York State he finished *A Glastonbury Romance* (which has been called the greatest novel of this century), and wrote *Weymouth Sands* and his *Autobiography* besides *In Defence of Sensuality* and *A Philosophy of Solitude*. Leaving America finally in 1934, he spent a year near Llewelyn in Dorset, beginning his novel *Maiden Castle*, before settling in North Wales, where he spent the rest of his life. He died in his ninety-first year on 17 June 1963.

Though a generation their junior, I am now growing old, and the writings of these two Powys brothers, along with those of D.H. Lawrence and Aldous Huxley, have meant more to me than the work of any other contemporaries. When my *Life of Llewelyn Powys*, on publication in December 1946, sold out its first impression in six weeks, it seemed that six years of wartime misery had opened peoples' minds and hearts so that they were ready to learn that life should not be wasted 'in a fretful utilitarian activity, with a half-satisfied acquisitive instinct as its high

INTRODUCTION

reward'—that 'the true purpose of life is personal happiness'. But the Atlantic Charter of Churchill and Roosevelt was soon shown to have been a mere stratagem devised to induce endurance of wretchedness in hopes of better things—hopes soon dashed by unprincipled politicians and industrialists. Since then we have run headlong downhill like a herd of swine to plunge into the pollution of cynical materialism.

There is time to pull out—at least for the young. Let them use this book as a springboard to leap into the habit of thought of these two great thinkers, and so learn to look inward in search of the good (or God) within themselves.

Malcolm Elwin

CONFESSIONS
JOHN COWPER POWYS

I

IT IS THE little thing, the unrehearsed gesture, the catch in the breath, the droop of the lip, the start of surprise, which really reveals. We may analyze ourselves in volumes and remain undiscovered; and then—by a yawn, a tilt of the head, a sob of exhaustion, a flash of hate—we are betrayed and unmasked forever.

It came over me yesterday that the whole secret of my being, of my happiness and my misery, was to be discovered in my *hands*. I speak as a biologist, not as a palmist.

Under ordinary conditions my consciousness does not penetrate to my hands. These curious human appendages remain inert, clumsy, helpless, heavy, dead. I have dead hands—the hands of a dead person! I cannot do the simplest thing with my hands without a definite and concentrated effort of will. It is like working with clumsy tools; tools that require elaborate direction every time. I cannot tie my shoe-strings, or post a letter, or light a match, without issuing a special mandate to my incorrigible hands.

That is why they are always knocking over things and dropping things and tearing things. They are out of the reach of the electricity of my being. My consciousness does not penetrate to where they hang, swinging so helplessly at the end of my arms.

When I am lecturing however—and this irritates my profoundest pride, for I despise the lecturing animal—my hands change completely and my consciousness flows through them to the tips of my fingers. They become sensitive then, abnormally sensitive. I *feel* them as I speak; and between them and the waves of my thought there is a direct magnetic connection. Under ordinary conditions my hands are the hands of a dead body. When I am lecturing they are the hands of a lover; of a lover caressing his darling!

Is that not a curious thing?—a little thing, but more suggestive than much analysis. The general public is certainly not any darling of mine; and yet when under the spell of addressing it my fingers become the fingers of a lover. This does

not mean that my emotions are kind. The
emotions of lovers are not always kind.

In reading what follows the reader must
be on the lookout for indirect betrayals
and unmaskings. He must follow me suspiciously, guardedly, furtively. He must
be prepared for that invincible human
trick of using language to conceal rather
than to reveal. I am ready to confess myself, as a man may be ready to throw himself into the water. But once *in* the water,
the instinct of self-preservation compels him
to swim.   So I swim—on words—unless
the reader's imagination is shrewdly alert
to thrust me down into the truth.

I should like to indicate here my recog-
nition, deeper than they believe, of the sublime patience of those who have suffered
from me. I make this signal as it were out
of thick darkness; for in spite of the sub-
tlety upon which I pride myself, I feel
vaguely conscious that I have been dull and
blind, in certain relations, as a twisted sea-
shell choked up with sand.

The more one tries to analyze oneself
the more one is conscious of amazing
paradoxes and inconsistencies which lurk
under the simplest surface. I think as

compared with most, I am strangely simple in my dominant tendencies. It is because of this simplicity that a certain duality in me becomes so disconcerting. I fancy sometimes that my exterior appearance gives an impression of power and formidableness that is altogether misleading. Below this Roman Despot look I conceal frequently a weakness, a shrinking, a timidity, an exhaustion of energy, a psychic disintegration of personality, natural rather to a slave than a master.

The only person as far as I know who has really come to believe in this abandoned weakness concealed under the mask of domination, is the admirable young painter Raymond Johnson, who in his mad picture of me—it needs a Post-impressionist to find out these things!—has compelled my material likeness to indicate the bewildered exhaustion of my soul. Perhaps it is because I have the soul of a slave that the great personalities, upon whose creations I lecture, have selected me among the rest as the most submissive medium for their revelations. Certainly they have a way of obsessing me as if they were so many demons.

There will be notes struck here and there in what follows, which will of necessity irritate and annoy many. I do not regret that: I cannot. In a profound and indescribable manner I feel that these things—these moods of almost vindictive rebelliousness—find their place and their justification in some underlying duality beyond the confines of rational logic. Criticism, protest, the will to destruction, even when exercised in frenzied helplessness against forces that *cannot* be destroyed, have their place in the world economy. The anger of the worm turning upon the universe may, in a larger synthesis, be nothing but the anger of one god with another god. And who can tell how necessary to the purposes of life are the quarrels of these immortals?

I have tried to indicate, in what follows, my most permanent reactions to the world; but the reader of these pages must remember that the river is flowing even while we are pushing our way across it and while there is life there must be change. I long to be an Epicurean; but something always drives me on, out of my pleasant cloister. I notice as a curious fact that many of the impulses that thus drive me forward are

my own maddest obsessions; and yet in
the violence of such pursuits I stumble
upon seashores flooded with moonlight,
and am rewarded for obeying demons by
encountering divinities.

II

I DO NOT think that anyone who has never tried the experiment of making a word-portrait of himself can possibly understand its difficulty. To achieve it with any success one needs one of two things; either an absolute and even ridiculous shamelessness, or a calm, imperturbable, psychological insight. The first of these requisites was possessed by the admirable Pepys, and in a less degree by Casanova and Rousseau. The second was possessed by Goethe, whose "Truth and Poetry out of my Life" is a masterpiece of analytical statement. The method used by Montaigne in his egotistic soliloquies is really a mixture of these two, with an added literary and epicurean unction which his peculiar temperament supplied.

But in all these instances, and in many others of a less famous reputation, we are conscious of one common element, at once the motive-force and the life-blood of such an enterprise. I am speaking of a certain

15

definite attitude of the person thus confessing himself, towards the self he is describing.

The nature of this attitude I can best indicate, by calling it a *sympathetic interest* in oneself. This "sympathetic interest" we find in all the famous confessions, from that of Saint Augustine to that of Oscar Wilde. Nor with the help of it need the humblest autobiography lack importance.

My own feeling is that any single person who ever lived, were he the stupidest on earth, could utter profoundly provocative things about himself—if only the necessary words could be conveyed to his intelligence.

I am not the stupidest on earth; though doubtless, compared with these great ones, my intellect is blundering enough, and my senses sufficiently dull. But were I the apogee of human incompetence, there would still, I maintain, be an immense interest available, if I could find words to hit the exact emotions and feelings which make me what I am. It is an insult to common human nature, this mock-modest Philistine notion that it is indiscreet and indecent for an ordinary person to attempt to give expression to his secret identity. It is really no more than a form of silly and vulgar pride to be so "cautiously reserved." It is evidence of a touchy, uneasy sense that if one did describe oneself, one would betray oneself, and shuffle off the pompous hypocritical mask with which one covers up one's foolishness. The "reserve" of which I am speaking is one of the most contemptible qualities of our English and American race. It is on a par with our fussy self-consciousness and grotesque "dignity;" a dignity which is only a parody upon the real virtue indicated by that beautiful word.

The natural, instinctive movements of Arabs or Latins or Indians never really make them ridiculous. It is we who make ourselves ridiculous by our stiff, jerky, spasmodic awkwardness. Reserve in social relations has undoubtedly its place—what could surpass the reserve of the Oriental?— but when an attempt is made to carry this social weapon into the sphere of literature and art, the result is only a general paralysis.

It is after all, as Goethe says, the *personal* which interests us. The attempt to substitute, for the personal, any degree of scholarship or erudition, is fatal to genuine interest, both in art and criticism.

There is a very widely spread view, current in educational circles, that what we call "introspection" is a dangerous and immoral thing, a thing from which our youths and maidens ought to be protected. "Let them look out upon the world;" such pedants protest. "What have they to do with analyzing and dissecting their own minds? Let them study the works of God, and cultivate their bodies, and be sensible and happy." This is all part of that unfortunate modern craze for what is called being "healthy-minded." Introspection and analysis are supposed to be a prerogative of degenerate natures, of natures that spend their time in useless brooding because they are inefficient in action. It is a grotesque mistake. One does not read that Socrates was less courageous because he had the habit of falling into introspective rances, nor does it at all appear that, in tthe present war, all the daring and efficiency is monopolized by the healthy-minded.

It is indeed by reason of this deplorable prejudice in favour of "reserve," and this ridiculous view that unreserved people are conceited and degenerate, that so little progress is made towards an intelligent understanding by man of his relations to himself. The most entirely reserved person that one has met—call him up in your mind, reader!—will probably be found to be the most conceited person one has met, and the most opposed to every kind of illumination. The fear of self-analysis is a cowardly fear, and suggests in the persons who betray it, that they have instincts and proclivities of which they are thoroughly afraid; and still more afraid of letting anyone else have the least suspicion.

There is of course a quite different type of reserved person, and a very sinister one. I mean the crafty, worldly-minded, predatory scoundrel, who habitually wears a mask, and keeps his thoughts to himself because they are base, narrow, greedy thoughts. A person of this kind is not conceited or unintelligent. He is only too clever. He plays up to the prejudices of the public and the moral hypocrisy of the preachers, with the most shrewd calculation. He despises the naive loquacity of unreserved artists and philosophers. He holds them as simple fools, who in place of quietly plundering the public and enjoying their little vices under the cloak of respectability, must needs go babbling forth into the street, and shouting out their secrets for the warning of all men.

Such an one has no time to regard his emotional or intellectual nature with "sympathetic interest." His pleasure is derived from the inward satiric glee with which he watches the stupidity of the sheep-like crowd, as he shears them to the skin.

A person like this is not necessarily a wonderful Napoleonic "blond beast." He is often more than a little stupid; and when thrown off the track of his economic depredations, will look like a plain fool in conversation with an intelligent man.

On such occasions his carefully cultivated reserve sometimes breaks down, and he gives vent to little barbarous absurdities, full of entertainment for the ironic observer. Entertainment one would no doubt derive from any observations such an one might be betrayed into making about this very sketch. Whereas a wiser rascal would only chuckle to himself under his beard because one more enemy of his class was "giving himself away" and incurring the malevolence of the mob.

"To write successful confessions one must regard oneself with sympathetic interest." This is my own statement; but I emphasize it again for a very important reason.

As a matter of fact, hardly any human being could be found, possessed of average intelligence, for whom the successful writing of confessions would be harder than it is to me. For I do *not* regard myself with sympathetic interest. This is indeed one of my most curious and personal characteristics.

I use the expression "successful confessions" deliberately, for I am fully aware of the ease and fluency, perhaps the too great ease and fluency, with which I can write some sort of a confessional sketch. By "successful confessions," however, I mean the turning of one's poor portrait of oneself into a true and permanent work of art; and it is that from which I fear I am fatally debarred, by my total lack of sympathetic interest in myself.

It will be found, I believe, if one reverts once more to the famous writers who have been successful in this branch of literature, that they all regard themselves with enormous sympathy. This sympathy may take the form of imaginative interest; or it may take the form of vivid dramatic self-consciousness; or it may take the form of tender sentimental pity; or it may take the form of humourous depreciation.

In every case however there is present a certain caressing tone of love and attraction in their attitude towards themselves. They love themselves well, in spite of all the derogatory things they say; and out of this love they create winning and provocative works of art.

I can almost conceive it possible for a person who hated himself, to make an attractive, though sinister portrait out of his detestation. But I—really abnormal in this—neither love myself nor hate myself.

The queer thing about it is that I am a tremendous and unconquerable egoist. I am pliable and unselfish in little things, but in main issues my self-assertion is monstrous. How then can it happen that I, who assert myself so vigorously, have no sympathetic interest in myself? I think the explanation, or one of the explanations, can be found in the fact that I pursue sensations so obstinately that I have lost all power of interesting myself in that thread of continuous consciousness, which, in our inmost being, binds our sensations together.

Sensations are continually taking me out of myself and away from myself. In sensations I forget myself; and if I did not forget myself, there would be so much less interest left in me to devote to sensations.

I am too much of a pleasure-seeker to care to stop and brood over my own being; though half the pleasure of my life is in brooding over the beings of those I love— the great artists and writers.

It would be different if I loved myself. Then no doubt I should be criticising and analyzing myself continually, with passionate pleasure. Am I, perhaps, the very acme and apogee of a born critic? I have been led, before now, into such a conceit; and even at this moment I do not regard it as an outrageous claim. I have this double advantage as a critic. My mind is singularly clear, fluid, and nimble; and my sensations are singularly detached, chaotic, and unclassified. I can therefore flow with

Protean agility into the minds and temperaments of others. I can *become* others and feel myself into their most recondite feelings; and I can do this with passionate pleasure and excitement, because I love others, while I do not love myself.

So many would-be critics are debarred from being interesting and thrilling in their discoveries, because they drag with them, wherever they go, their devotion to themselves and their own ideas. I am free from this burden, because I have no devotion to myself and no ideas of my own.

Side by side with this clear, transparent, unclouded, flexible mind, I have a great many strong and tenacious sensual prejudices. It is necessary to have these in order to write interesting and exciting criticism; for criticism is nothing if it is not extremely personal. In my criticism I am at once abnormally impersonal, and abnormally personal; and that is why I may turn out—to resume my old conceit— to be one of the best critics in the world. My impersonality springs from my complete lack of convictions, opinions, principles, or any system. My personality springs from the inveterate obstinacy of my sensational prejudices, and from the curious absence among them of any connecting imaginative link. I am, in fact, as a critic, naturally objective and naturally subjective: objective, because I become with unclouded, fluid preciseness, exactly what my author is: subjective, because my separate sensations so completely occupy and obsess me. It would be true to say that I live, in a very narrow sense, a double life. I live in my mind, which is eternally restless, mobile, and light as air; and in my sensations, which are heavily-weighted, earth-bound, and obstinately unchanging. It is no fantastic abuse of language to say that my sensations are chaotic; for though they are so fixed and indelible, they are not in any way connected with one another. They have no intelligent continuity, no symbolic orientation. They are not fused or moulded by any shaping imagination.

Mental detachment and sensual detachment—that is the form my life takes; and that form is a *cul-de-sac* or *impasse*, when it comes to any question of "improvement" or growth. My sensations cannot grow because they have no living principle of life in them, no imaginative vision, no emotional concentration. My mind cannot grow because like a floating film of white mist, it takes shape and colour from every single one of the peaks and promontories which it passes in its erratic wayfaring.

I present therefore the appearance of the most sceptical as well as the most obstinate of men. And this appearance coincides with the reality. My life is made up of the passive reception of alien ideas, and the passive assertion of inalienable prejudices.

I believe everything and—nothing; and I pass from sensation to sensation like a moth from bush to bush.

III

I SAID I had no ideas of my own; and I have none. But the reader must not think me inconsistent, if, all the way through the following pages, he comes continually upon references to Fate. The impression of Fate is not an idea; it is a fact. It is an inevitable human category. It is understood by instinct and propitiated by superstition. It is like the air we breathe and the ether that surrounds us. It is impossible to escape from it. It is the great Truism, the eternal Axiom. It is the thing originally "given," the primal stuff of all our experiences. Every philosophy, every system, every idea, has, as its main difficulty, the problem of dealing with Fate. A belief in Fate is neither a philosophy nor a system; it is a necessity.

But though this is true of the impression of Fate, I may perhaps go so far as to admit that the peculiar quality of my mind—its colourless receptivity—lends itself in an especial sense to an understanding of Fate's implications.

An unconquerable scepticism in the sphere of every explanation of this fact, tends to throw the fact itself into forlorn prominence. I may also admit that my predilection for what is chaotic and disconnected, for what is arbitrary, perverse, and exceptional, springs in like manner from the irrational and incalculable nature of my detached sensations.

From what I have just said—and the mere saying it chills me with the shadow of myself—it is perhaps made a little more clear how difficult it is for me to paint a vivid portrait of such a subject. I am not, in myself, an attractive subject; though the impetus and magic with which I can interpret the attraction of others is so prevailing, that many, in coming to know me as I really am, must suffer serious disappointment.

It is not only strangers, and such gentle, unknown sympathizers as may be led to read my writings, who are thus disappointed. It has been my ill-luck to lead into devastating disillusion some of the most charming friends I have ever had. They too have judged me by the swift Protean transformations, by which I have the power of assuming the very tone and temper of the writers I love.

They too have been interested and arrested by the significant intensity of my original sensations. They too have looked anxiously for the imaginative vision that should give these sensations coherence. But such a vision, such a coherence, has never appeared; and they have been thrown wearily back upon the spectacle of an insane sensationalist, pacing, like an imprisoned tiger, round and round the same cage; and of an insane sceptic, losing all identity and personality and substance, in airy diffusion into empty space. It is impossible for me to blame the faithful friends, who, thus provoked and tantalized beyond endurance, turn and rend me with bitter speeches. I sympathize with them, and not with myself. I love them, and not myself. And yet the crafty obduracy of the accursed thing I am, grins patiently at their indignation, smirks an ironic assent to all they say, and shuffles off to behave as badly as ever.

In one very curious point I have absolutely deceived many simple people. I have the power of suggesting the existence of abysmal gulfs of "wickedness" in a deep and terrible soul. I am led sometimes almost to the verge of self-deception in this matter. Even now I confess I cannot quite explain how it is that certain of my emotions, which I feel are really on the surface and purely a matter of that border-land between the brain and the nerves which we call the "psychic" region, should seek to present themselves to me as if they uprose from unfathomable depths and were, as we say, *inspired*.

It must be due to a self-deception of this kind that the idea of the Devil first took possession of man's imagination. I have been ridiculously tempted now and again to assume the Luciferian cloak and stride forth as a kind of poetic Manfred, ravaged by scoriac scars.

How much more exciting I could make this quiet sketch, if I gave way to these prompt-ings and indulged in hints and suggestions of dark evil profundities in myself of which I was the Satanic victim! But I am too sceptical for this, and my mind is too clear. Ah! how vain and foolish show all such fuliginous hallucinations, in the presence of the marble countenance of Eternal Fate!

I know well enough that my darkest, most anti-social instincts are nothing but the pure material accidents of some pre-natal jolts and agitations, of some trifling pathological chances of birth and inheritance. It is when the imagination invades the mind that it is able to play such pranks and build up its elaborate metaphysical illusions out of what are pure material twists and warpings. My imagination is as completely detached from my mind, as my mind is detached from my senses. That is one of the reasons why I find myself so unlovable and unattractive. I am, as it were, a loosely-tied knot of sense and mind and fancy; and the resultant fabric is too unraveled to be agreeable to handle.

My imagination could play me, if my sceptical reason were not so detached from it, all manner of quaint tricks. It could persuade me, for instance, to turn this harmless little work of patient analysis, into a most formidable and lurid picture.

Led by it I could enlarge upon certain of my inherited vices, until, all my life, off the immediate track of these dangerous obsessions, became like a drunkard's sober interludes, dull, colourless, and lethargic.

It could persuade me to take possession of some one particular vice—a mere accident of birth—and thrust it, with awe and terror, into dark mysterious caverns of primeval being, until it became like the smoke of Hell. It could provoke me to turn some accidental perversity into a great spiritual tornado of evil, making a desolation of all it touched.

It could easily do any of these things; and it has come near to doing them, when, for some cause, my wandering, irresponsible mind has deserted its post. But it never has really done them: it never has really had its way with me; because my obstinate, incoherent senses, and my airy, fluid reason, are very difficult things to dominate.

I sometimes feel as if I were a dead body, galvanized temporarily into performing the necessary functions of existence, but only inspired with real passionate life, when some great spirit from the past, some Epicurus or Spinoza or Goethe, touches me with his magic.

It is an odd thing this feeling of deadness, of heavy material inertia. It is combined in my case with the teasing pricks of a thousand annoying thoughts—thoughts of practical difficulties, of hypochondriacal apprehensions, of social antipathies; and it weighs upon me, for hours together, more heavily than my harassed stomach. It is not only the great souls from the past who can cry aloud to this corpse that is I, "Rise up and walk!" I can be drawn back to life by the vivifying presence of any brave and joyous companion. Given the society of one person that I know, my second self, my "brother in the Lord," and I could pass an eternity of earthly days without ever falling back into myself. He would feel for me; he would laugh for me; he would cry for me; and with him I should become a natural living person full of buoyancy and friendly grace. With him by my side, life would become to me like the perpetual reading of an exquisite book —some unending Marius the Epicurean or Jean Christophe—the pages of which I should turn every day with new delight and wonder.

Perhaps my peculiar disposition is one that was really intended by nature to be so accompanied. Perhaps, shorn of this solace, I really move through this world atrophied and stunted, inchoate and paralyzed. Perhaps it is the want of this "alter-ego," of this "twin-soul," that makes me turn so wearily away from normal humanity, and grow so dull and morose. Perhaps it is the want of him that lends to my little absurd vices their obsessing quality, their preoccupying importance. I know well enough that, when I am with him, my vices are as nothing.

If it is difficult for me to write this brief dissection of "the body of my thought," it would be far more difficult for me to attempt anything of an autobiographical nature.

I cannot bear to recall my childhood; and those memories of youth which bring tears of sentimental self-love to the eyes of the most hardened, fill me with nothing but a cold repulsion.

My past self, at any remote epoch, seems so unpleasantly like my present self that I loathe to think of it. In fact, in many respects, I prefer my present self to these clumsy caricatures, these shuffled premonitions. By long practice I have learned the art of escaping from myself. After blunderings and absurd experiments,

I have discovered what particular authors, and artists, and people, and places, are best adapted to save me from myself.

My whole life has been one long running-away; and years have given me swiftness and agility. I am now such an adept at self-forgetfulness that I might almost claim to be able to jump over my own shadow.

I should not be giving an absolutely faithful sketch of what I am if I did not allude to a certain quaint and strange phenomenon which sometimes confuses me by its appearance. I allude to the phenomenon of "possession." If any man has been the victim of this ancient experience, it is surely I. I am sometimes, it would seem, literally "possessed." Now it must be understood that I do not for a moment believe in any supernatural object corresponding to these experiences. I believe them to be entirely explicable on purely material grounds; but I should be false to myself if I did not confess that, when they appear, they appear accompanied by the illusion of spiritual reality.

I have suffered at different times from the presumption of three distinct "possessions." Under the influence of one, I become insatiably "wicked," and have the illusion of wickedness as a thing of infinite horizons and possibilities. My sceptical reason mocks at this formidable nonsense, and hints satirically that the whole thing is due to some trifling chance of pre-natal warping.

Under the influence of another, I become preternaturally "noble," and have the illusion of "goodness" as a thing of infinite horizons and possibilities. My sceptical reason mocks at this too, and points to the atavistic presence of some blind race-instinct which would fain submerge the selfishness of the individual in the loftier selfishness of the tribe.

Lastly, and most curious of all, I have a splendid and transcendental "possession," under the influence of which I feel conscious of an invincible courage and an unconquerable contempt; a courage ready to look all accidents, all chances, all circumstances, in the face, with calm indifference; a contempt that rises magnificently above both good and evil, and feels itself the initiated accomplice of the abysmal mysteries of life and death.

I am quite aware that these experiences are not peculiar to me. I have a shrewd suspicion that all the children of men come under this influence at one time or another. I think, however, that the abnormal receptivity of my temperament makes me especially liable to them, and it is for this reason that I offer myself to psychological analysis as a particularly emphatic type.

This sketch might be made much more interesting and effective, if I set out to project a deliberately imaginative dramatic figure, such as I could wish to be, such as I could myself contemplate with love or pity or admiration. But such imaginative projections, to be convincing and touching, require a life-long training of the self-conscious mind. Such projections are, as a matter of fact, what artists and artistic-minded people naturally do evoke. They mix their imagination with their senses, and their senses with their reason; and upon the resultant amalgam they throw the inspiring torch-flame of some great symbolic purpose. They do not stop to ask whether they are on the right path, the path justified by objective truth or by material reality: they just steer boldly forward, and in unscrupulous, pragmatic excitement create, or half-create, their own "truth."

As I shall endeavour to show later, my own attitude to these people is one of ingrained contempt. I despise their imaginative projections, their artistic, pragmatic pseudo-truths. I am all for the bare, bold, merciless determinism of drastic conformity with fact. It is very quaint—the way I feel in this matter. For, of course, among the great artists, who are now dead and buried, and whom I love so well, there must have been many who played fast and loose with their pleasant dreams, just as these moderns do.

And yet I am not sure. There seems a certain affectation of artistic attitudes common to our generation, from which the older masters were free. Or is it only that, being so near to them, their little ways are more annoying? I do not know. I only know that it is absolutely impossible for me to make an attractive work of art out of the contemplation of my own moods.

This sketch resolves itself, then, into what I should be inclined to claim as one of the most cold-blooded dissections on record, of a living person by his own hand. It is incomplete, because the opinion of our day is unprepared to welcome absolute candor. But as far as it goes, it is drastically sincere. It is meagre and dry and sapless. But it is this because, apart from the special outward objects that inspire me, my mind is meagre, and sapless, and dry.

To the question "what use then in publishing such a depressing document?" I should answer at once that the value of the thing is strictly psychological, and, as such, of immense and suggestive interest.

Given an eloquently impassioned critic, —and not even my enemies could deny my right to that title—it is, I maintain, of curious and delicate interest to know what the texture of such a critic's mind is like. I am always engaged in analyzing the minds of clever artists; let me for once, undertake the less pleasing task of analyzing the mind of a clever critic. Incidentally such an analysis is bound to throw a certain interesting light upon the relations between criticism and creation.

After all it is perhaps just as well that the temper of the public should have made it impossible for me to do more than allude to any of my peculiarities which may be anti-social or antinomian. It is so easy, if once one begins dealing with one's more sensual attributes, to be led into the most fantastic exaggeration. One requires a touch as light as a gossamer seed, and as penetrating as a gnat's sting, to follow into their elaborate intricacies the sensual proclivities of even the most guileless among us. And after all, what most of us would be tempted to undertake, if we entered upon such an enterprise, would be an indication, with wanton flights of fancy, not of what we have ever done, or are likely to do, under the existing pressure of circumstance and situation, but of what we could conceive ourselves doing, if this or that obstacle were removed; an obstacle which we know very well, never in the nature of things, can be removed; an obstacle which would probably turn out to be our own tenderness of heart, or timidity of spirit, or temerity of conscience.

I have not indulged in descriptions of how I feel in English country gardens, as compared with my sensations in the corridors of American hotels; or how I feel in the presence of crowded audiences, as compared with my emotions in the solitude of a railway carriage: for these things are not really germane to the matter. What I have attempted to do is to sum up as clearly as possible, the most salient and persistent of my instinctive reactions to the general drama of the world; and my most inveterate and obstinate attitudes to men, to nature, and to the unknown.

And there seems to emerge from it all, for me at least, the image of a nervous, timid, morbid, but at the same time, reckless, figure; a figure full of quaint anxiety to be loved and admired, but utterly unable to love or admire itself; a figure troubled and perverted by strange obsessions; a figure blinded by obstinate pride, yet crippled by ridiculous humility; a figure grotesque and comic, but not devoid of elements of forlorn distinction; a figure fleeing across an interminable desert to escape from the shadow of itself; a figure half-dead and atrophied, yet responsive as a reed to celestial harmonies; a figure driven forward by Fate, yet pathetically seeking to love the Fate that drives it; a figure fettered and bound by sensual infirmity, yet mocking with subtle derision every ideal that would liberate it; a figure struggling beneath the burden of its wretched contradictions, yet looking for no issue from its dilemma, save in the narcotic power of critical analysis, and the obliterating power of death.

For out of the ghastliness of the historic cataclysms which surround us now, there must sooner or later be a return to the cultivation of our own particular gardens; and my "garden of oblivion," until I die, can be nothing else—of that, at least, I am sure—than the memory of great men and the interpretation of their labours.

IV

I HAVE no Philosophy; not even the Philosophy of having no Philosophy. By this last remark I mean that my scepticism is genuine scepticism; not, as so often happens, a mere synonym for dogmatic agnosticism. I do not construct out of my scepticism any *system* of universal doubt.   I doubt even the validity of doubt. I hold myself perfectly free to dally with any kind of metaphysical or mystical interpretation of things which may happen to attract me.   I hold myself free to give myself up, in passing, to any religious revelation that may strike my fancy.   I hold myself at liberty even to play with what is called "Faith."   Let me try to put down, point by point, how these evasive ultimate tendencies really do present themselves as I disentangle them.

I think it may be said that though no rigid exclusion of idealistic interpretations closes absolutely any door for me, my general bent is towards what is roughly called materialism. I say "roughly" called, because I am not ignorant of the metaphysical and psychological dilemmas implicit in any rigidly monistic system. But at the same time I have never been able to see that the *spiritual attenuation*, if I may call it so, to which what we roughly name matter has been recently subjected, necessarily implies any support to the claims of the idealists. The world may be full of mysterious living forces; it may have a boundless tendency to burst out here and there into all manner of conscious forms and shapes; it may be prolific of amazing organisms; it may be deep and strange and unfathomable; it may possess levels beyond levels of cosmic entities and inconceivable beings; it may dwindle off into unthinkable spatial planes; but I can never bring myself to see why this quite possible multitudinousness of life's pregnancy should be dragged in to support the obviously human-made systems of idealistic or religious comfort. The world may be as deep and mysterious as you will, but that does not in the least imply that *we* shall have a life after death or that there is a God, whether personal or immanent, in the least concerned with *us*. Perhaps what I feel about it is rather what the ancient Epicureans felt. There are, very likely, gods and demi-gods innumerable, in life's teeming planes of existence, but their own pleasures and their own annoyances are quite sufficient to fill up their time.

I am not therefore a materialist in the dogmatic sense, but I lean, considering the important part played by what is conveniently called matter in our human sphere, to a materialistic view of our own particular fate. It is in fact upon the inscrutable mysteriousness of the world that I take my stand. I find myself constantly protecting, as it were, this large and tremendous mysteriousness, against explanations which seem to impair its dignity. This is no doubt the origin of much of my prejudice against current theology. It is certainly the origin of my profound suspicion of current science. I want to keep the fresh, formidable, beautiful virginity of the world, if I may be allowed to put it so, unravished by priest or professor. I feel so often as though that indescribable quality which the poets call magic, were in danger of being destroyed by these cut-and-dried idealistic assumptions. The dignity of death is, for instance, absolutely spoiled for me by easy arrogant hopes of joyful resurrections. Even the great Buddhistic theory of successive incarnations seems to me less *poetical* than the finality, touched with a remote just-articulated chance of "something else," of the tragic pagan "*ave atque vale!*"

It is really, I fancy, on behalf of this dramatic mysteriousness of things, with its astounding fusion of comic and tragic elements, that I reluct at committing myself to any clear-cut solution. I think it is also because I feel certain that no solution will prove the final one. I experience indeed a curious anger against certain clever modern philosophers whose crafty reasoning lends itself to the comfortable uses of optimistic apologists. "If such people as these 'I say to myself' find support in such theories, then such theories must be wrong!" Yes, at the bottom of my mind I discern an instructive and inevitable assumption that no theory of the universe which anybody has ever had, or will conceivably ever have, can possibly be true. As for the popular Hegelian idea of

progressive evolutionary truth, I despise
and deride it. The ultimate secret is as
far off now as it was in the time of Heracli-
tus, and I have a suspicion that all who do
not confess this are either knaves or fools.

I do not carry my scepticism so far as to
doubt the existence of what we call "objective truth." Such an extreme of the
personal method seems to me grotesque
and insane. Besides, carried to its absurd
limit, it renders all conversation between
intelligent beings impossible.

Some definite and unalterable relation
between the human mind and its natural
surroundings must be a permanent thing
in our planetary history, otherwise we
should be condemned to the "incommuni-
cable muteness of fishes."

Pluralism is a pleasant theory to play
with, and perhaps has its place, but I
must confess that the indissoluble unity of
the world of which we form a part is borne
in upon me as an axiomatic necessity of my
consciousness. The universe may have all
manner of layers and levels of divergent
life; its fluctuating waves of being may ebb
and flow through incredibly varied spheres;
but one cannot formulate in thought any

gaps or blank spaces there, not connected by some sort of delicate ethereal medium. The universe must remain a universe while our mind remains our mind. To call it a "multiverse" is to use language which makes language impossible.

The same thing applies to the rationality of the world. There must be processes, sequences, harmonics and laws in Nature, binding all things together, and more or less intelligible to us, the children of their creation, otherwise no kind of science would be possible.

Though I am so anxious to keep the virginal mystery of the world fresh and unravished, I am not now addicted to talk loosely and lightly about the "chaotic element in Nature." I used to talk in this way; but I think it was rather an impatient reaction against idealists than any expression of my own personal feeling.

I have a rooted prejudice against all syntheses which smell of the pulpit, and it is pleasant and consoling to me to think that though there is evidence enough of law and solidarity in the system of things, there is not the slightest evidence of such a system being guided or evolved to any definite end or purpose. Even if such evidence were forthcoming, it would still remain extremely improbable that in the vast cosmic orientation, whatever it might be, there should be any particular consideration for our human wishes and cravings. However well the universe may be constructed, and however harmoniously Nature's laws may work, one sees clearly enough that a certain monstrous and lavish *waste* is an intrinsic peculiarity of the whole system. And of this waste, of this essential cosmic negligence, *we* may be a self-deluding infinitesimal portion.

Nature may have her own mysterious purposes, or she may not; in any case our rôle is bound to be, in a dramatic sense, that of the fly upon the wheel; or to use a more organic metaphor, that of the lice in the hide of the rhinoceros.

There has been too much nonsense lately talked, about things being free, arbitrary, individual, and independent of one another. I myself, reflecting the prevalent fashion, have uttered vague words about the "chaotic multifariousness" of the world. I have made much of every trace of the illogical, the exceptional, the perverse. I have sought to discern the presence in things, of something incalculable and baffling, of something that suddenly leaps up without preparation or any apparent cause, out of the depths of the Uranian reservoirs. It is for this reason that it used to please me well that the modern philosophical catch-word should be "Life," rather than "Matter" or "Motion" or mechanical "Force" or than that old unpsychological figment, "Mind" in the abstract.

"Life," though it might not carry us far, seemed, or I said it seemed, much more suggestive than any of these others, as a focusing word for the ultimate mystery; for it had the advantage of emphasizing the unique, arbitrary, and *personal* element in what is presented to us.

It will be seen from all this that when I spoke of my preference for what I called the "chaotic" in life, I was using the word in the sense of something that was wayward, wanton and incalculable, not in the old Miltonic sense of pre-created debris and dust. I blush now to think how far, in my casual conversations and lectures, I carried this absurd belief that things were "chaotic," and this fantastic preference for such a world. Nothing could be really further from my true feeling about the universe. Nothing could be further from my wish as to what the universe should be.

I must have been betrayed into this treachery to my own disposition by some species of proud and mischievous spleen, and by an unconscious following of literary fashions. As a matter of fact these "chaotic" forms and shapes, these sudden groupings and miraculous chances of contact, though they seem to have about them all the arbitrary magic of the unknown depths, and to be quite independent of the uniform procession of cause and effect, are really as much a determined part of the whole inexorable stream of things as the most mechanical sequences.

Though there be world within world of spiritual or ethereal entities, they are all equally dominated by destiny; they are equally driven forward by the same universal impetus. The smallest fancies that pass through our brain, and the strangest, remotest inhabitants of the farthest star, are alike determined in their nature by a fatality that admits of no interruption or deviation. This does not in the least debar us from giving ourselves up to the exquisite imaginations of artist and poet. Such imaginations are also part of the irresistible unfolding of what has been implied from eternity. We do not know how far they will carry us. We do not know how far our own thoughts will carry us. But both they and our maddest dreams are all accounted for in the terrible, beautiful procession of lives and thoughts;—the procession of things and the shadows of things, which is all there is, and from which there is no escape.

We may use what in our necessary illusion we call our "free will" to the utmost extent. We may struggle, we have a right to struggle passionately, to change our nature; but our nature will never really be moved one hair's-breath from what has been determined for it, and every one of our vaunted new thoughts and new emotions has really been inevitable from the beginning. If we struggle desperately to "improve" or change; that very "will to struggle" was what the universal destiny implied in us; and if we do not struggle, that atrophy and inertia also was what the universe intended.

I once fancied that I shared with Bergson and James—those plausible sophists!—a predilection for the "instinctive," over the "logical;" but I now know, falling back upon my real feeling, that it is neither instinct nor logic that can save us from the inexorable pressure of life's fatality. It is quite in harmony with what one experiences in the daily commerce of events, that nature should be, at the same time, driven irresistibly forward, and *apparently* prone to a thousand goblin-like absurdities. It *is* prone to absurdities: these are not only apparent—they are real. But proneness to goblin-like absurdity is part of the universe's inherent necessity. The universe is both fated and fantastic. One can see clearly why it should strike us in this double-edged manner when one thinks of it as completely indifferent to our personal desires; for just in proportion as we desire fluidity and malleableness, it arrests us with its granite-like immovable weight; and just in proportion as we desire security and stability, it leaps out at us with wanton and ironic capriciousness.

This astounding mixture in the system of things of rigid cosmic laws and apparent chaotic surprises is precisely what pleases my aesthetic sense; and the sardonic shocks it gives, on the one hand, to optimistic rationalism, and on the other to optimistic pragmatism, fill me with humourous satisfaction. I cannot help it if any gentle spirit protests that such an attitude is one of pure malice. I am not defending myself. There *may* be malice in it. There may even be a touch of perverse voluptuousness; possibly an absurd element of pride. If so, I can only look with amazement at myself, and observe with psychological interest the odd spectacle of a human being deriving voluptuous and humourous pleasure from the pathetic inability of other human beings to grasp the mystery of life.

As a matter of fact, I am convinced that *all* philosophical attitudes are the result of temperament. Generally the part played by reason is the part of defending and supporting, as cunningly and persuasively as possible, this initial bias; but in certain rare cases it happens that a philosopher summons his reason, not to defend his temperament but to outrage it, lacerate it, and contradict it. In such a case we have a system of philosophy, based, not upon the pleasure the philosopher gets from offending the natural tastes of others, but upon the pleasure he gets from offending his own.

But even here, though so perversely employed, the man's temperament is at the bottom of his method. I do not think, however, that my philosophy is of that kind. At all events I recognize it as a profound tendency in myself, to sweep aside the plausible structures of logical thought which philosophers raise, and to dig down with curious psychological zest into the personal will and taste and prejudice of the philosopher himself.

For me as I have hinted, the world of human beings, their character, their predilections, their love and their hate, is a world fatally, and rigidly determined; and that is probably why I deal so habitually in patient and ironical agreement, and find it so hard to indulge in argument or controversy. My underlying Spinozism, if I dare call it by so ambitious a name, probably accounts also for my indifference to detail among the exacting transactions of life, and my tendency to let things drift as they will. Why make a fuss, when all, at the last, is equal?

But beyond and below Spinozism, or any other fatalistic method of reasoning in which I may love to indulge, lies undoubtedly in my own instinctive conviction that "nothing matters," that there is no real *human* meaning in life at all, and no beginning or middle or end of life's teeming manifestations. All is equal. Those sinister syllables keep up a sort of recurrent tune in the depths of my mind. All is equal. Why then grow agitated and angry because this or that ridiculous human being acts according to his nature?

It is no doubt out of a sort of willing reaction from the sombre inertia of this mood that I love to "dally," as I call it, with the more gracious aspects of religion. Innately I regard religion—the Catholic Church for instance—as a noble and beautiful work of art, constructed anonymously by humanity for its own satisfaction, and offering a lovely and romantic escape from the banalities of existence.

I am not in the least troubled by its inconsistencies or impossibilities. If it were not superbly impossible, if it did not come flaming in, from outside the closed circle, it would not be worthy of the name of religion. A rational religion is a contradiction in terms; and only thoroughly stupid people are interested in such an anomaly. The value to me of this wonderful impossible invention having appeared at all upon the earth, is the fact that its appearance makes one consider once more, how extremely likely it is that the real truth of the universe is something amazingly, absolutely different from anything that anyone has dared to dream. Religion at any rate must always have this value, that it prevents our self-satisfied men of science from closing the door to staggering chances.

As the supreme work of art of our race, I have the utmost reverence for religion; and as a protest against barring out incredible possibilities, I regard it with admiration. When however it becomes a question of possessing "faith," or having what is called the "religious sense," I must confess to a cold and complete indifference.

One sometimes hears worthy people express the view that Atheism is an impossible thing; that there can be no such person as an Atheist; and that those who call themselves so do not know their own minds, or are deliberately indulging in fantastic bravado. I can never understand this view of the case. It seems to me that I am meeting Atheists every day; that is to say people who are not endowed by nature with faith or with the religious sense. For myself I can only say that, however deeply I search my heart and soul, I do not find the remotest trace of these interesting gifts. Nor do I feel as though I had permitted such instincts to perish in me through lack of cultivation. I do not feel as though they had atrophied from disuse. I feel as though they had never been there. I certainly cannot remember them; though I can remember very vividly certain disgustingly hypocritical attempts I made at various times to pretend to myself that they were there. This fact, the fact of one tolerably sensitive person being entirely devoid of the religious sense, is surely not without its significance. It at any rate disposes of the argument of the universality of the instinct.

I should be untrue to my attempt at getting really to the bottom of my emotions in these things, if I neglected to speak of the curious thrill which the idea of the Person of our Saviour always produces in me. I notice that this thrill only occurs when it is accompanied by the notion, as it naturally is with me, of His Divinity. That idea of a great good Sage going about doing admirable works and finally giving up His life for humanity, leaves me absolutely cold. I even feel an odd sense of anger when I hear worthy ethical rationalists talk, as they do, of "Jesus and Socrates." That sort of thing freezes my interest like a bucket of ice-water.

I suppose it is the artistic instinct in me, indignant at this clumsy and stupid lack of appreciation for the most wonderful work of art our race has ever evoked. It is precisely the attraction and magic of this Figure, created a God by the mysterious self-mesmerism of the human race, which causes the thrill which I feel. A merely good man, possessed of an unusual love for humanity, does not particularly impress me. I do not love humanity myself; and I do not feel any particular sympathy with those who do.

I am ready to confess, as a proof of my sincerity towards my religious friends, that

I cannot altogether explain the thrill I have referred to. It resembles in character the feeling I have when I read an especially magical line in poetry—the only moment which ever gives me the sensation of tears. Is it an atavistic thing, I wonder; a reversion in me to the mediaeval emotions of my ancestors? Or is it a purely artistic impulse? I refuse to call it religious, because it is not connected in the remotest way with any need or desire to worship. It certainly is not moral, because I have often experienced it when I was about some deed "that had no relish of salvation in't," and it has been accompanied by no shadow of remorse or scruple.

Before leaving this interesting borderland of philosophy and religion, I want to say a word about the absence in me of the mystical sense. I know no human being less of a mystic than I am. In this matter my irreverent and sceptical "materialism" —if that is the best word to describe it— goes to the extreme limit. Fancies about an over-soul in things, or an "anima mundi," always rouse in me images of a comic kind. I see the universe as an enormous sponge; through which the "spirit," or whatever they call it, pours, seething and fermenting, like cider out of a vat. The "something far more deeply interfused" of the Wordsworthian ecstasy leaves me contemptuously frigid. I am tempted to give to this great pantheistic emotion the grossest and most material causes. I am always driven to associate it with animal feelings of purely physiological well-being. I was not born to be a Pantheist. The idea of worshipping God in Nature, or worshipping Nature as God, has never had the remotest appeal for me. My instincts are all Polytheistic. A quite unmystical and perfectly naive worship of the sun or the moon or of any particular planet, is the sort of thing that I understand and sympathize with.

I know what is meant by the phrase "cosmic emotion" but I never feel it. What I feel is a perfectly natural and sensual enjoyment of a particular field, or flower-garden, or river-bank, I do not want these things to lead me to the brink of Heaven or to the feet of God. The spiritual raptures of Shelley's ethereal inspiration please me as poetry, but in practice a curious vein of humourous and cynical realism holds me bound to the earth.

In these things I am frankly and grossly material. What appeals to me in Nature, what gives me always the most thrilling delight, is what one has learned to call the *magic* of her fleeting and evasive charm. This "magic," however, has nothing to do with hidden ethical secrets, or with hidden spiritual depths. It is not hidden at all. The whole wonder and beauty of it is that it is on the surface. It comes and goes. It allures and escapes. The appeal it makes is not to the mystical sense, but to the poetical sense. It is the amorous witchery of the earth-maidens and the irresistible laughter of the earth-gods.

V

PASSING from religion into the world of moral problems, I am especially anxious to make my real attitude, as it wavers and flickers, as clear as possible. It is here that one is especially tempted to make the best of one's "little ways," and to round off, with a show of consistency, moods and impulses that are at the bottom absolutely inconsistent.

And yet how interesting it were, if the most ordinary of human beings could be persuaded to analyze and set down, with genuine unscrupulousness, his real moral experiences!

It were surely a matter of some psychological importance, perhaps even of some ethical importance, if a person could bring himself to state frankly where, and at what points, his own private conscience moves in agreement with the social conscience, and where it deviates from it and pursues its own road.

I suppose that, in the last resort, I must be what they call a Hedonist,—that suspicious-sounding name which made Pater wish that everybody knew Greek. I suppose that, ultimately, I pursue Pleasure— and Pleasure alone—as the chief end of my cults and activities. The poignancy of the situation, as far as conscience is concerned, begins to assert itself for me at those points where my Pleasure conflicts directly with the Pleasure of other people. Until some point of this kind is reached, I am absolutely devoid of scruple. My line of thought and action may run dead contrary to the conscience of the community to which I belong, without my experiencing the least discomfort of soul. I may think and do things absolutely under the ban of the current ethical code, and my conscience will remain gay and unruffled— it will even feel a certain agreeable tickling of pleasant self-approbation.

It is when my pursuit of pleasure crosses, with a direct impact, the instinct of self-preservation in others, that the pinch comes. I am, by disposition and taste, fatally aware of the existence of these other people, of these alien egoists in my path.

It is as disagreeable to me to rend and maul them, as it is to break the branches of delicate trees or to pull up the roots of sensitive flowers.

An egoist myself, I know well how egoists suffer when their particular life-illusion is interfered with, or their particular aesthetic vista blocked up. And every man, woman or child I meet is an egoist for me. I suspect them all of living ultimately for nothing but Pleasure—even as I do. They may talk of duty, and self-culture, and the service of humanity, and the will of God—I seem to waive aside all that, and perceive under every mask the old eternal pressure of the life-lust.

It causes me much inconvenience—this conscience of mine; many sacrifices, many wretched unillumined hours. I sometimes hesitate on the brink of envying those thicker-skinned, more impervious scoundrels, who go ahead mercilessly, and strike out for what they want even across the bodies of their friends. But I never do really envy them. I think I have an instinctive feeling that the same imperiousness in them, which makes such indifference possible, causes them to lose endless exquisite emotions of pleasure to which my less unruffled skin remains porous and sensitive.

Thus I am one of those who would never be able, unless under circumstances of intolerable aggravation, to leave a tiresome friend or companion, and lash out for liberty at every cost. To cut difficult knots by "quitting," as my American moralist recommends, is out of the question for me. I must not claim too much virtue. It is probably not merely my dislike of giving other people unpleasant shocks, but my dislike of receiving them myself, which restrains me.

I am naturally averse to any kind of drastic action. In fact I dislike all action, whether drastic or otherwise. My atavistic reversion, if we all do really have so quaint a thing, is towards the passive, rather than the predatory world. I suppose my ideal existence, out of the human circle, would be that of some happy iridescent jelly-fish, expanding its sunlit body in placid warmth at the bottom of a rock-pool, hurting nothing and being hurt by nothing—and living entirely for sensation. Apart from the jelly-fish, I find the life of a Prairie-

Bison a very desirable one. Lizards in the desert seem also enviable; and there is much to be said, to my thinking, for the innocent role played in this life-medley by the lichen upon an apple-tree, or the moss upon the roots of an elm.

This singular reluctance on my part to strike out and mould, as they say, my own life, is connected I fancy with every one of my profoundest instincts. I cannot endure the idea of giving people violent jerks and blows. I cannot endure the effort, the action, the dealing with material difficulties, that such movements require. I long for things to change; but to change things, one has to have the energetic will-power of a demiurge; and there is absolutely nothing demiurgic about me. I like the sensation of being "created." I do not at all like the responsibility of "creation." I am always sceptical too, about any change. There are bound to be people and things, wherever I go, clamorous, obtrusive, and demanding some kind of response. Custom has made the things I am used to, more easy to handle. I have acquired the tricks of my own burrow, and know how to avoid the barking dogs and the men with guns. If I go forth into new fields, the chances are that I shall encounter much more noisy invaders of my solitude. What is called "travelling" always implies Policemen, Inspectors, Custom-House Officers, and Government Officials. It often implies Bandits and Brigands. An individual with a nervous dislike of his fellow-men, were wise to remain at home. I may go far in search of quietness, and after all, discover no path so unfrequented as the one I have learned to find the way to, from my own back-door. I have acquired by long experience the art of moving among turnips and mangel-wurzels; why should I go stumbling forth to find cactus and deadly night-shade?

My unwillingness to march forth to liberty over the bodies of people, is further accounted for by a quaint fear I have that I may suddenly discover depths of affection and tenderness in me that I never suspected. One would feel a considerable fool if one sacrificed "love" to "liberty," only to find oneself in another kind of prison, and "love" murdered at the gate. One never can tell! One cries aloud for freedom, and strikes down this or that barrier, only to fall into some devilish gin far more murderous than the last. To preserve the liberty of one's thoughts,—that at least is something! While one can go aside in lonely places and mutter one's weariness of flesh and blood into the ear of the elements, one's lot is not hopeless.

Apart from my fear of unsuspected depths in my affections, I am prevented from deserting my post by a much less admirable quality. I have, to confess the truth, an absurd desire to be regarded with fondness and complacency, if not with respect.

To be considered a hard-hearted ruffian, by parent or wife or child, would be extremely disagreeable to me.

One curious and most fortunate gift I owe to my good genius. I have absolutely no pining for what is called "spiritual affinity." I have not the least objection to living with people of divergent or even opposite tastes. In the abstract, I cannot even regard such affinity as a thing to be desired. It presents itself to me as a spiritual invasion, as a rushing-in of alien waters into my sequestered harbour; as something troublesome, exacting and confusing.

I like being myself and going my own way, and I like my companions to do the same. Such contrarieties afford an opportunity for me to indulge my predilection for irony, for psychological analysis, and for living a double life. I despise people who must always be receiving sympathetic assent to their ideas. I do not want sympathy. I want kindness, fondness and affection.

All that I have just said applies to my habitual feeling about spiritual affinity in the abstract. As a matter of fact, in one single human case, I have had the good fortune to know the pleasure of such an affinity in actual experience. In this case I did not ask for it, or seek for it. It just occurred. And I am bound to confess, at the risk of being held inconsistent, that it has turned out one of the great felicities of my life. Is it necessary for me to add that this startling interrupter of my method, this bold subverter of my abstract theories, is one of my own sex?

No: with regard to matters of conscience, I am extraordinarily unwilling to over-ride my friends, or cause them shocks or inconveniences. I continually go out of my

way, and worry myself with teasing burdens, for their sakes. I sacrifice the main
object of my life to them, that is to say my
Pleasure; and I land myself in situations
that necessitate what I detest above everything else, that is to say *action*. Lest this
should be regarded as a monstrous boast
of virtue, I hasten to add that it only applies
to little external things. In the larger
issues of life—short of moulding great
events and inaugurating new departures—
I generally get what I want; and I get
it, not by any elaborate Machiavellian
schemes, but by a certain pliability of
nature which makes it possible for me to
bend like a reed, without ever breaking.

My egoism has its own perfectly unconscious and instinctive arts which reach
their end by the most devious and unexpected paths.

I am naturally much more sympathetic
with the physical sufferings of people than
with those of a moral kind. I always regard
physical suffering as an outrage, as a scandalous anomaly, as an insult to the harmony
and pleasantness of life. I am not one of
those who think that we gain by suffering
and become nobler. According to my ex-

perience, people lose by it and are hampered, stupified, mutilated, distorted, and embittered. In this matter of physical suffering, my conscience does not only work negatively; it works positively. It runs into very extreme excesses. It becomes what many persons would call "diseased."

This is the cause, among others, why I can never bring myself to eat the flesh of oxen, sheep, and pigs. It is not that I object to their being killed. It is that I dislike extremely the manner of their killing. If people went out into the pastures and gave these innocents pleasant little electric shocks that caused them to fall instantaneously dead in the midst of their browsing, I would eat them with avidity.

The same thing applies to Socialism. My conscience compels me to be a Socialist, and I suppose I shall always be one; though none could dislike more than I the idea of being interfered with by a stupid set of moralistic Bureaucrats.

I have no prejudices in the matter of political freedom. I listen with humourous contempt to the inane chatter of Democratic Idealists. I would resign my political rights to-morrow with absolute equanimity if some great despotic commission of Kitcheners and Roosevelts could settle the matter of poverty once for all, and arrange that everybody should have the pleasures of life, and be well-fed, warm, and contented. I prize liberty as much as any. In fact liberty is the breath I must breathe. But I would willingly submit to serious curtailment of the invaluable thing, if by so doing I could relieve my conscience at a stroke of this uncomfortable background of responsibility for the abominable miseries which we inflict on the poor.

It is in things of this kind that my conscience pricks and plagues me. In other matters, where there is no question of giving people or animals direct discomfort, I have no conscience at all. In realms of comfort outside the question of causing suffering, I do exactly and precisely what I please, limited only by motives of expediency. This sounds wonderfully heroic and antinomian; in reality I shrewdly suspect it is very much what everybody does: for I notice that the human conscience is more alert in condemnation of others than punctilious in self discrimination.

And when one comes to examine into the matter, what an enormous mass of so-called moral restraint is purely an affair of expediency! Certain lapses, certain wanderings from the path, seem to us best avoided; not in the least because the current morality condemns them, but simply because, given the circumstances we are in, they would lead to troublesome situations and embarrassing complications. Take the virtue out of the world which is the result of pusillanimity and caution, and how much would be left?

For myself, I can only pray that I shall always find it wise and expedient to be sweet-tempered, friendly, considerate, and amusing; rather than sour, irritable, heavy-handed, gloomy, and dull. For, in the last resort, it is the happy and gracious people who make life tolerable, and the sulky, touchy, ill-conditioned wretches who poison its pleasant hours.

At the same time I must confess I would prefer to spend my days with an irritable egoist who possessed genius, even though he made life extremely inharmonious, rather than with a cheerful fool who could do nothing but amiably chuckle. This however is a matter of taste. As a general rule, then, my conscience is quiet and flexible. Economic injustice, the disgusting slaughter of animals, brutality of parents towards children, vivisection, harshness to prisoners, are the only things that really rouse and excite it: though I am conscious of remorse when I inflict upon my friends the discomfort of my moods of animal depression, or the moroseness of ill-health.

VI

To turn to a completely different aspect of one's life; I suppose it would be impossible for any human being to be more absolutely under the dominance of Literature than I am. I think by books; I move in an atmosphere of books; I am an infatuated bookworm. To the influence of books I have come lately to add the influence of Art; but it is Art approached through books, interpreted by books, and loved for bookish reasons. This obsequious submission to Literature and Art follows naturally from the morbid receptivity of my nature. It follows too from my curious dislike of self-assertion, and my weary desire to "lie back" upon something or other external to myself. I love books and pictures, just as I love Fate. They are something upon which I can lean; something in which I forget myself and lose myself; something in the presence of which my clumsy and turbulent identity melts and grows lucid, flowing, transparent. This "too, too solid flesh" of mine "thaws and resolves itself into a dew" when brought near to these delicate influences.

They satisfy also my deep-seated and inveterate longing for Romance, for something that shall lead my spirit far away from the accursed commonplace, and send it sailing free over distant horizons.

I hate and loathe the commonplace; and yet because of my abnormal receptivity, the commonplace invades and stifles me more abominably than any one thing I know. Certain vile concentrated incarnations of the commonplace especially seem to arrest and paralyze me. Such is the effect of that horrid moment after mid-day lunch; when, in any decent English establishment, one is desolately conscious that the unfortunate servants are all gathered at the sink, washing odious greasy dishes. Such is the effect of those bleak, littered, fretted hours of miserable waiting, when intolerable visitors drag on their inane "conversation," and one watches in a kind of petrified torpor the cups of lukewarm tea and the photographs on the mantelpiece.

At such times a mad "receptivist," such as I am, suffers misery beyond words.

Lucky indeed are those happy people whose nervous skins are thick enough to endure these bleached hours and their withering negations without experiencing a sensation as though their heads were going to burst. Such happy people have the power of lolling interminably on sofas and couches when there is no one there who is beautiful, and nothing there that is exciting, and no discussion there that can rouse the remotest tinge of interest. Much of this sort of thing would literally drive me out of my wits and send me, with the King of Babylon, to eat grass in the pastures. I am especially adapted to be the half-suffocated victim of the commonplace because my damned consideration for other people prevents my lashing out and taking myself off; and my yet more accursed receptivity throws me stripped and helpless into the horrid moment's maw.

Artists, excellent drastic egoists, can strike out and be merciless. They must have their little attics and studios to themselves, or they will roar like ten thousand bulls. But I, poor receptive madman, absolutely lack this shrewd creative energy in the midst of the materials of life. I am as helpless under these blighting social siroccos as a bear tied to a pole.

I seem to have a pathetic idea that I have only to remain passive and quiescent, and all the perfumes of Arabia will float through my senses. Instead of which, what floats through me is the withering, devastating breath of every commonplace person, and object, and thought, and belief, and ambition, that our wretched race has ever evoked.

It is out of the utter paralysis of misery which the invasion of the commonplace causes me, that I cling so desperately to Literature and Art. Being at once so wretchedly receptive and so absurdly romantic, and being at the same time so devoid of the aggressive creative faculty, I turn to Literature and Art as my one grand escape.

In exciting stories I can forget my vexatious plight, and sail away down lovely rivers of enchantment, quite oblivious of people and things. In poetry and philosophy I can see the world transfigured, and even learn the secret of that exquisite lie which would make me believe that the commonplace itself is wonderful and charming—if only one looks at it from a certain angle. I confess I have never been able to find this angle. But it is a relief to be told that it is there.

It is curious that I should, in my general feeling about life, demand a certain drastic realism with certain stern, abrupt unmitigated edges; and yet require Art and Literature to protect me from reality when it is near at hand. The truth is that, in the background of my Picture of Life, I like the grey formidable skyline of austere, unblurred, unsoftened fact; while in the foreground, and even in the middle-distance, I like the tender, deceptive colouring of literary association.

This is because I feel that in ultimate things, the facts of the situation are more mysterious and terrific than any artist's dream. I wish to protect them from artists' dreams. I wish to keep them untouched and impenetrable. It irritates me to see these artists and poets project their impertinent personal fancies upon those granite walls.

But when it comes to the "little things of life;" when it comes to the immediate world of commonplace persons and ambitions, then, by all means let us have the artist's imaginative creations, and give them full play! Let us have the lover's, too; and the priest's, and the philosopher's. Let us have even the sensualist's. Let there be a general conspiracy of exquisite Fantastics, against this bleak and horrid domination. Let all things be seen through the magical blurring mirrors of Literature and Art.

Through these two mirrors, I, at any rate, see everything that comes near me. Some people have accused me of being deplorably dramatic and theatrical. This is a mistake. I am only dramatic in a literary sense, and only theatrical when my theatrical attitudes have received a literary consecration. There are plenty of people naturally dramatic and born with a mania for dramatic situations, who are not literary at all. I have, I confess, a palpable weakness for dramatic situations, but they must have that deeper, richer, more *continuous* atmosphere of literary pungency about them, to make them really my true element. I am dramatic; but not melo-dramatic.

This tendency of mine never to see anything directly as it is, in clear objective transparency, but always through some kind of heightened medium, has at different times proved very irritating to my companions. Why cannot I, they say, interest myself in a thing's actual shape and colour and texture? Why cannot I search out in it the impersonal rhythm of Nature and her subtle mathematical laws? And with people and situations too; why cannot I grasp them in their natural independence? Why must I always be dragging in memories, associations, and personal prejudices? Why does not the beauty of the clear-cut reality suffice me, without blurring it and disfiguring it with the oblique mists of sentiment and fantastic romance? Why cannot I, even for a moment, forget the drama of my own sensations, and become a clear camera-plate for recording the truth? Why, in a word, am I always so hopelessly subjective? Well! I have no defence to offer—no reply to make. I can only say that thus, and not otherwise, have the blessed Gods created me; and thus, and not otherwise, I shall be to the end. I am the slave of books, the slave of sensations, and the slave of my unfortunate "receptivism."

Nothing is more interesting than to lay one's finger on the false hypocritical gestures into which at times nearly all of us are betrayed. I do not profess to be able to unmask myself at every point. Our power of self-deception is deep as the salt sea. But I think I have noticed one most curious piece of pretence in my habitual procedure, which I will hasten to expose.

It is this. In my writings and lectures I continually advocate a certain elaborate epicurean cult—a cult of sensations and ideas, deliberately undertaken with a view to deepening and intensifying one's vision of life. I speak tenderly and passionately of this premeditated art of making the utmost of every drop of Time. I speak of the epicurean pleasure to be derived from the least and most ordinary events of every day—its food and fire, its sunrise and sunset, its felicitous groupings, its chance encounters, its fortunate omens, its gifts of comedy and tragedy, its sacramental and symbolic burden. I speak of a deliberate refinement of our powers of appreciation and understanding; of a deliberate cultivation of our consciousness, so that it should embrace more and more of the rich and astounding spectacle offered to our enjoyment.

I talk of this art of lingering delicately by the way, tasting everything as it passes in its sweet confusion, and committing one-self to nothing, as though it were an art I myself followed in my own life, and wherein I were a master and adept. As a matter of fact I am the very opposite of all this. The above is my doctrine,—the doctrine I have drawn from my favourite writers; but my practice is the extreme contrary. Certainly I follow Pleasure; but anything more different from my way of following it, and the wise, deliberately or-ganized way recommended in what I speak and write, could hardly be conceived.

Here—and it is an interesting psycholog-ical fact—I fall completely away from my conscious philosophy. I fall back upon the unconscious in myself, upon moods and im-pulses which spring up independently of any art of life.

According to my philosophy, it were wisdom to balance one sensation against another, and to connect them all reasonably and intelligently, like precious beads, upon the silver cord of my self-consciousness.

My doctrine is that I should let *nothing pass*, and abstract the lovely quintessence and delicate pungent flavour from every single one of my common hours.

But what in reality do I do? I plunge madly about, from hunting ground to hunting-ground. I sink desperately into this obsession, into that vice. I let the most gracious moments go by utterly un-remarked as I plan and plot the satisfaction of some absorbing desire, some ill-balanced greedy wish. Of course even here my innate tendency to touch life indirectly, rules and prevails. A certain type of book, for in-stance, becomes a vice to me, and I read madly, frantically, savagely, everything else shut out, until a violent reaction comes, and I would fain bury the accursed thing at the bottom of the deep sea.

It is curious how one can be inconsistent with oneself, and yet profoundly consistent. Even in love-affairs it has been my exper-ience to find myself combining this tendency to treat things as if they were alcohol or drugs, with this other tendency to be in-direct, evasive, sentimental; and to drag in remote fantastic comparisons.

It is the same with beautiful foreign cities, their squares, churches, streets, pictures and canals. My critical friends catch me hanging on bridges, loitering in gardens, standing at gaze in cloisters and alleys; and they say they observe a sort of drunken sensuality in my absorbtion, as if I were one of Poussin's amorous Satyrs bending over a sleeping Nymph.

It is perfectly true that I have a curious predilection for certain fabrics and materials. Everybody has, I suppose; but I must have a way of accentuating and obtruding my tastes, and turning them into perversities and intoxications; otherwise my friends would not be irritated by such harmless fancies.

I certainly must confess to extremely strong sympathies and antipathies in the matter of places and scenery. Sometimes these run strangely counter to accepted notions of the desirable. Mountains, for instance, dear to nearly all lovers of the picturesque, seem to be nothing but depressing top-heavy excrescences, bulging forth from the kindly earth's smooth surface, and keeping the sunshine and air out of the dwellings of men.

Huge cataracts, vast rivers, enormous lakes, jagged, cataclysmic crevices, and titanic canyons, are all detestable to me and full of desolation.

My favourite scenery is the sea-shore, especially when there are vast stretches of sand there, or wide salt marshes.

After the sea-shore, I prefer sandy volcanic plains, with an occasional abrupt hill crowned with olive-trees and one or two solitary cypresses. Damp fields, damp woods, damp foliage, damp over-grown gardens full of damp ferns, are what I dislike most of all. They make me cry aloud for the desert.

Rains and storms devastate me. Why could not the Creator have dispensed with these discomfortable interruptions to conversation? I certainly feel no inclination to worship "Him that rideth upon the Wings of the Wind." My God is a God who sits serene and silent, under great moon-lit palm-trees.

The thought of the large free expanses of the desert, whether in its hot noons or under its glittering stars, makes me realize what it is that I require from natural scenery. I require an escape. I require an escape

from all disturbing and distracting objects
—objects and people. I want to be liberated
from everything that "sticks out," from
everything that calls attention to itself by
its colour, its form, its challenge.

Civilized scenery is classical and nobly
monotonous. It is a background to the
distractions of beautiful cities, beautiful
people, and beautiful works of art. Gothic
scenery is different. Its hills and rivers,
its rocks and chasms are always clamouring
to be noticed, to be admired. They are
always saying "Look at us. Worship us.
We are the wondrous works of God."

The civilized beauty of the desert and
sea-shore makes no barbarous claims of
this kind. Here one can forget every disturbing object, every disturbing emotion.
The universe is adored here under one
symbolic element, be it sand or water, and
there is no mortal thing to separate us from
the horizons of air and sky. I confess I
derive a certain misanthropic and Spi-
nozistic pleasure from seeing things thus
reduced to the ascetic minimum of form
and colour. With nothing but the sea or
desert before one, the planet falls into its

place, and the primitive necessity of the elements throws life and its concerns into due proportion.

VII

I T IS A natural transition to turn from such contemplations to the contemplation of personal extinction. Death! I should like to set down, if I could what I really feel about death. I think I have as little objection to death as anyone not in actual physical suffering. Perhaps it is from a certain inherent and constant tiredness, both mental and physical, which never leaves me, that I look upon death with so little dismay. Perhaps it is also because I lean so strongly to the idea of complete annihilation. I notice that the people who fear death most, are the people who believe most intensely in another life. And this is quite natural. It is their passion for life that makes them so credulous. I have no passion for life, and I regard death as an escape from a thousand annoyances. Don't let me be mistaken. I am the reverse of brave. It is not valour but cowardice that makes me look upon death so often with weary satisfaction.

It is the fault of my temperament. I am so made that I feel more vividly than others the innumerable pin-pricks and vexatious responsibilities that every day brings. I am always being driven into action, and action is detestable to me. I look with immense pleasure upon the hours when quietly in my grave I shall not be called upon to *do* anything of any kind at all.

Hatred of action is at the bottom of my character. And yet I must have change. These two antipathies together, the antipathy for doing things and the antipathy for remaining in the same place, are the dominant motives of my average mood. I have absolutely no sense of possession, no love of property. I hate my books, my pictures, my furniture, my garden; and I even feel sometimes antagonistic to the charming view from my windows. I was born nomadic, anarchistic, deracinated. I can write decently when I am in hotels, inns, railway trains, and foreign cities. If I am to do anything of the kind "at home," it must be in a room bare of every object, and with white-washed walls. The nearer such a room approaches the austerity of a cell or a barn or a shed, the better work I do.

My chief objection to living in the country is that one eternally sees the same hills and roads and fields, and the same people. The last place on earth where one can be alone and unrecognized is in a country village. Every dog, every cow, every sheep, every pig, every fowl, and every blackbird, seems to think it necessary to greet you with a cheerful personal salutation. And as for one's neighbors—dear, gentle hearts!—one cannot forget them for a moment.

You will say that if I have such a passion for change, it is strange that I should like sea-shore and desert better than woods and fields. The point is that these pure ascetic elements, these world-materials reduced to the minimum of simplicity, satisfy my desire to escape from objects and things. Woods and fields are very obtrusive objects. They are always growing leaves and dropping leaves, or growing flowers or dropping flowers. They tease one with their claims and insistencies. They have the exuberance of human acquaintances. Pet animals are the worst of all; especially dogs, those incarnations of pathos. Cats I endure very well, and even confess to a sneaking fondness for them. They remind me somehow of the irresponsible desert. They look as if they had just come from sitting crouched for a thousand years at the feet of the Pyramids.

I suppose my craving for change is really not so much a desire to be somewhere, as to be somewhere *else*. I have grown weary even of Rome and I can remember a fretting longing to turn my back on Florence. Venice of course is the city of my heart; but I can imagine myself wishing bitterly never to see a lagoon again.

Before I pass from these general aspects of my feeling towards life, I should like to revert once more to the moral problem. I am above all anxious to analyze to the very bottom my objection to optimistic views of the world. Is this pride? or is it an attenuated and sublimated form of the voluptuous pleasure one sometimes derives from a sense of power over fragile and delicate things? The universe is not fragile or delicate, but many people's pleasant illusions about it are most certainly so. Is this one of the reasons why I require a universe that shall be at once ruled by necessity and ruled by chance? Perhaps I really want the prospect to be devastating to the ordinary person's temperament. Perhaps I really say in my heart "if the ordinary person and his spiritual comforters crave a friendly universe with a God behind it— then I will disturb this faith!" Perhaps I really say "if the ordinary person longs for a malleable universe, a universe that we can make what we like of,—then I will disturb that faith too!"

Do I, in fact, want a universe that shall annoy the mystic by its incurable levities, and one that, at the same time, shall annoy the pragmatist by its fatal austerities?

No! I cannot quite believe I am as wicked as all that. What, then, are we to suppose is the true origin of this curious desire for a pessimistic interpretation of the world? Let me suggest an aesthetic origin; for it cannot be that I want delicate and sensitive souls to be outraged in their hopes. I am no devil. I want sensitive and delicate souls to be thrillingly and exquisitely happy. What I do not want is that any arrogant individual thinker should be right; or, still less, that the vulgar complacent optimism of the popular poets and preachers should have any justification in the facts of the real case. Perhaps behind my wish that the universe should be whimsically perverse for the benefit of the rationalists and rigidly rational for the benefit of the pragmatists, lies really a desire to keep the thing large and weird and outrageous and lovely; to keep the thing, in fact, the huge, grotesque, impossible, mysterious enormity which it is,—a thing eluding all general solutions, and thrilling us while it slays us.

This question, of the real nature of my dislike of optimistic interpretations, whether such interpretations be rational or instinctive, is a question that I think goes very deep. I think it goes to the very bottom of my soul. It is no doubt closely connected with another tendency of mine, which has met with reprobation at various times; I mean the tendency, in criticising any well-known author of ambiguous or antinomian proclivities, to throw these proclivities into vivid relief, in place of softening them or smoothing them down. The same tendency has been observed in me by unkind observers, even in the matter of ordinary conversation. "Why does the fellow"— such caustic observers have been led to exclaim—"why does the fellow rub his hands together and gleam with satisfaction as soon as any blasphemous explosion or erotic outrage is referred to, while otherwise, as we speak of worthy people's harmless ejaculations he sits dull and spiritless like a toad upon a log?"

Now what peculiarity is it in one's nature that leads to this perversity? May it not be a dramatic instinct, craving the stir and excitement, the stimulus and provocation, which powerful emotions of an abnormal character alone can give? And does not the presence of such an instinct in us suggest that a world devoid of this austere and sinister complexion would be a very depressing world, a world from whose rational excellence one would long to escape?

The whole question of our attitude towards what is usually called "evil" is a profoundly difficult one. Subtly intermixed with a vigorous and direct condemnation of certain things that instinctively strike us as evil, is a large and queer toleration of many things apparently regarded by the world as deserving that sinister name.

Does this only mean that we, in our hearts, are naturally of the company of the lost; or does it perhaps imply that, working through conscience, the human race itself is advancing to a larger, a nobler, a more generous and natural view of many problems?

However this may be, I am quite ready to admit a very close connection between my scepticism in regard to ultimate interpretations, and my lack of severity in regard to many moral issues. In my deepest heart I lean, as I have said, to the view that, when we die, our "souls" die with us, though I do not, as some are inclined to do, close the door absolutely to other possibilities. I say "other" possibilities, not kindlier possibilities, because I must confess that my more general feeling is that the dead are to be envied, and that annihilation is no "appalling stroke." This is said in all quiet seriousness, as I habitually feel it, and in no mood of bitterness and bravado. I do not revolt against the universe because, like Saturn, it devours its own children. It does not in the least depress me that death should end all, or that I shall never meet again those I have loved. All will be equal then: and those who have made life exquisite for us will be with us still, loved and lovers together, under the gentle river of oblivion.

I agree, from the profoundest depths of my being, with the opinion of the great Schopenhauer, that suffering, of one sort or another, is a more noticeable and persistent thing in life than any happiness or joy. Our pleasures come and go, like swallows touching the surface of a stream, but the waters of unhappiness flow on without pause, swift, dark, and deadly.

It is perhaps this underlying sense of the inherent discomfort of life, and its strange beauty, that leads me to feel a certain weary indignation with those who would interfere with the few golden hours which fate allows to us all. I think perhaps it is just there that I would draw the line of my own ethical code. People who by their unkindness, by their gloomy selfishness, by their spiteful vindictiveness or peevish jealousy, darken and discolour the days of those whose fate it is to live with them, seem to me bad people. I condemn them and struggle against them; and am favourably disposed to all who are their enemies. I never feel the least scruple of conscience in helping the victims of these people to escape from their clutches. They are the accomplices of everything that makes life intolerable. They

are themselves the leaden heart of its
burden. Rough, coarse-grained, over-bear-
ing tyrants, despots with more will-power
than intelligence, and more intelligence than
sensitiveness, these are the beings my soul
loathes and my moral sense condemns.
Passionate criminals, murderous criminals,
I regard of course with natural apprehension, but I feel no spark of moral anger
against them. In cases of lynching, my
sympathies are always with the person who
is being lynched.

As for thieves, forgers, bandits, and other
enemies of society, though I have a selfish
disinclination to fall into their hands, my
moral sense remains quite unstirred by
their depredations. I am even sometimes
tempted to fancy that they take back no
more than what is their own. "All property," as the Frenchman said, "is robbery;"
and though, being no saint, I cling fiercely
enough to my spoils, I am no hypocrite
in my sense of possession. I do not regard
myself as superior to the wastrel because
I have had the luck to inherit hoarded
plunder. Between me and the tramp there
is nothing but the difference of pure chance.

VIII

THE READER will have recognized by this time what I am trying to do in this personal sketch, and he will not, I trust, be angry with me for omissions which were originally implied in the method I have adopted. What I want to do is to give a picture of a certain type of character thrown upon the world, and of its struggles to adapt itself to inevitable circumstances. The margin of possible re-adaption in everybody's life is necessarily small; the longer one lives, the smaller one sees it to be; but the value of such a sketch as this, apart from its psychological interest, lies in the warning it may give, to other, younger temperaments of the same type, to guard and protect themselves under similar difficulties.

The important thing, it seems to me, is to recognize fully as quickly as possible both the limitations of one's own disposition and the limitations of one's circumstances, and to lose no time in adjusting one's self-assertion to these moulds. How many hours have I not wasted in trying to be something else than what nature intended! How long it is before one really discovers what nature did intend! I was born for sensations, rather than for action. I was born to enjoy sensations, to analyze sensations, and turn sensations into verbal and literary rhetoric.

A person whose philosophy of the world has been corrupted by his morality, would at once rebel, in angry disgust, at such a destiny. He would force himself to engage in manual labour; he would force himself to undertake the support of some great social reformation; he would assume every practical responsibility he could lay hands on; he would regard his incompetent sensationalism with shame and aversion, and by drilling, by gymnastics, by methodical activity, and the avoidance of sensational lures, turn himself as far as possible into a healthy-minded, energetic and useful citizen. I refuse to regard such drastic methods as right or wise. Is nature so poor a mother, is life so meagre a theatre, that there cannot be found scope and opportunity for so harmless an abnormality as mine?

Do not suffer yourselves to be depressed or paralyzed or converted, dear companions in sensationalism, by this stupid Public Opinion. Nature, not Society is your parent; and you may take my word for it there are ways and means of drawing upon natural forces that will make you strong enough to fight Society on quite equal terms. The revolt is much more extended than you suppose. You are not alone in Israel. You have only to focus your scattered energies, to concentrate your drifting emotions. The instinct of self-preservation in the Life-Stream itself, requires your self-assertion. Nature will never suffer the strenuous or the practical to work a final victory over you.

But to return to my self-analysis. I am certainly, of all men, the most helpless and incompetent in dealing with what we call "matter," with material obstacles, material complications, material embarrassments.

In the presence of the simplest material difficulty—I am positively ashamed to give examples—I am struck helpless as an empaled snake. I wriggle, head and tail, and utter inarticulate expostulations. No one can believe the misery into which the most obvious practical necessities plunge me. My hands are made for nothing upon earth but explanatory gestures. They refuse to obey any practical command; and the rest of my body is as helpless as they are. I have not the mechanical skill necessary for the simplest undertaking.

Little absurd physical imbroglios render me completely hors-de-combat. I can neither ride, nor climb, nor dance, nor shoot, nor fight, nor drive, nor whistle, nor hum a popular catch. I would sooner go without food for twenty-four hours than face a savage landlord, or order a dinner at an improper hour from a sulky head-waiter. To quarrel with an official or a policeman is an impossibility to me. To differ in opinion from a stern fellow-traveller is a nervous effort quite beyond my reach.

I cannot refrain from wondering what would be the effect upon me of a little wholesome military training. I suppose if I survived the experience, I should be a different person. But though I have no liking for myself, I do not want to be a different person. I want to remain myself, with certain obstacles and infirmities removed, and my own respect gained.

Probably I shall end by perishing like Turgeniev's oratorical Rudin—shot through the heart in an attempt to analyze his last revolutionary sensations.

I am afraid I am appallingly well adapted for the hero of a sarcastic light comedy. I sometimes fancy I must present myself to my friends under the guise of an elongated penguin, if the reader recalls those queer polar amphibians, with their incompetent flapping appendages and their eloquent gestures. I do not know how penguins make love, except from vague reminiscences of Anatole France's story. Moving Pictures of polar latitudes seem to omit such details; but I sometimes fear that in that final proof of practical heroism I am as much of a fool as in the rest.

I suppose it is by reason of this physiological clumsiness that so few female penguins —of our race—have ever regarded me with anything but distant interest. The youngest of young girls like their friends to be smart, well-dressed and enterprising. I have been very severely taken to task for an awkward blunderer, even in the art of innocent flirtation. Perhaps it is out of a kind of revenge for these rejections that my wayward fancy loves to imagine queer impossible situations in which such exacting young persons are led to beg very pitifully for my Sultanic commiseration.

I keep calling myself a "sensationalist," but let it be clearly understood that I am the very opposite of a Sybarite. My sensationalism is of an imaginative cast. It leads me constantly into absurd extremes of asceticism. I am naturally an ingrained ascetic, with lapses into luxuriousness. What is called "comfort" has very little claim upon me. Many of my most exquisite sensations demand discomfort as their appropriate accompaniment. I must however indicate that even in my avoidance of comfort I am abnormally and unhealthily aware of the material aspects of things. I am superficial. The surface of existence constantly obsesses me. I cannot forget it in the stream of great emotions. I suppose the only occasions when I do forget this obtrusive "matter" and all its little exactions, are when some wonderful line of poetry, or some astoundingly imaginative picture, lifts me out of myself.

Sometimes, though less often, philosophical analysis has the same effect. In analyzing things, I escape from them. In dissecting them, I rise above them. I would indeed recommend to everybody, who like myself suffers from the pinch of life's material engines, the wisdom of this procedure. Nothing in the world remains uninteresting when the analytical intelligence is brought to bear upon it. This is really what Spinoza means by the liberating power of the understanding.

I suppose a not unimportant revelation of a person's life, and one not unilluminative as to his character, is the sort of advice he would give—were he put upon his oath of seriousness by the presence of death or some tragic calamity—to young people inclined to lend him their attention. One talks in ironic disguises to one's contemporaries and elders. One usually hates them so that one wants them to remain exactly as they are. But it is a different thing when it comes to youth. O youth, youth! May my tongue wither in my mouth if I ever insult thy sweet docility by false conventional maxims or vain jocular bravado. Youth is the hope and salt and salvation of this muddy, brutal world: and those who refuse to take youth seriously, be they as clever as Plato or as subtle as Hegel, are surely deserving of un-mitigated damnation.

For myself, the one thing I fancy I have a genuine right to be proud of, is the fact that when I have to deal with youth I grow scrupulous, considerate, serious, and grave. I do not say that I grow responsible.   My very anxiety not to make a mistake renders me extraordinarily unwilling to assume responsibility.

I am so afraid, too, of interfering.   How many impertinent parents and other conceited elders take upon themselves to push young persons here and there; to plunge them into this profession or that profession; to mould and maul and mangle their tentative tender self-development!

It is in this matter of the education of youth, that I find myself differing from many of my free-thinking friends, whose views I otherwise endorse.   They seem perfectly willing to thrust down the throats of these sensitive fledgelings all their original theories and ideas.

I cannot feel it in this way.   In solitary conversation with any child, who wants really to know what I think, I express myself as gravely, exactly, and minutely as I should do if I were holding a sort of Judgment Day Dialogue with my own soul.

But I never imply that my personal opinions carry any more weight than the child's own. I avoid the ex cathedra manner. Indeed I am at pains to make it clear to my young friend that I am myself only attempting to justify by reason and argument what remains at bottom a matter of personal temperament. With this in view, I do not shrink from presenting myself to him as a "queer fellow" or one who has his eccentricities.

Beyond this, I am inclined to put the child in the way of outward conformity with the customs of the country. I let him see that I myself, go my own way, irrespective of these customs, and then leave it to him to develop, under the surface of their convenient cloak, any individual rebellions he may be led to adopt, out of the pressure of *his* personal peculiarities.

If the child is naturally extremely sensitive, it is better that he should be impressed by the flexible, easy, *outward* conventions of immemorial usage, than that this or the other individually-thinking person should warp him with his private prejudices.

In all this I am largely influenced by my inherent scepticism, and my invariable suspicion of the value of every kind of private judgment and personal conclusion, including my own.

It is this sort of sceptical, ironic acquiescence in timeworn usages that I should indicate to the child as the safest road. And I would always suggest to him the advisability of suspending his judgment upon many problems until he is older.

I would gradually communicate to him, in fact, my own attitude towards these ancient conventions, but I would present my personal ideas in so light a way, that he would not be bound to take *them* any more seriously than those of the Community.

Nothing is more repulsive to me than the manner in which certain earnest-minded parents fill their infants' heads with their own pompous heresies, and make odious little conceited free-thinkers of them. The great art of successful education according to my view is to protect the delicate minds of children from the imposition of the self-willed private opinions of their elders. And this is done most successfully by putting them under the exterior formalism of some ancient time-worn system, especially when the healthy-minded paganism of the child is fortified by a little carefully instilled sceptical doubt. Children are much more subtle and intelligent then one supposes. With the least encouragement they will quickly be found to steer clear of any premature committal of themselves to this or that profession or opinion or party. They know as well as we do that they are feeling their way; and they often quite consciously make use of the thousand and one distractions of childhood to protect themselves from our untimely meddling.

I remarked, in connection with the cool manner in which we genteel classes sponge upon the wage-earners, that I was not enough of a saint to give back my inherited plunder to the armies of the homeless and unfed. That is true; but, for all that, I have a queer inexplicable penchant for a saint's life. How lovely to possess nothing, and to have no ties! How lovely to wander about from village to village, living on bread and milk, and working miracles! One peculiarity, usually noted in saints, I already do possess: I have a genius for making a fool of myself. It is an interesting psychological phenomenon—this role of being a fool. There is in it much more malice than is usually supposed. One sometimes does it simply in order, in a queer perverted way, to be *revenged* on the proud, well-constituted people one is forced to meet. But I do it, maliciously too, I fear, in my relations with my friends. I exaggerate my eccentricities; I parade my adversities; I expose all my most secret and scandalous thoughts. I love nothing better than to be the butt of my friends' ethical and intellectual indignation.

I sometimes defeat my own ends however at this little game; for though I begin doing it in order to lead the darlings of my soul into the sin of pride, I not infrequently end by feeling really as if I were a kind of moral abortion. And this feeling is less agreeable to me than might be supposed.

I referred just now to the sin of pride. I wonder if I am proud, or, still worse, conceited? I think perhaps I am; for, when it comes to the point, I get hardly any exultation of feeling from the things I can do, such things as talking, analyzing, criticising, interpreting; and a great deal of exultation from a vague belief in the possession of much higher powers, powers to be displayed to the world some day, but at present extremely deeply hidden. Is it not grotesque that I should still have the illusion—it is not an illusion to me—that I have the power to write really important and original poetry? Should I not have done so already, if I were destined to do so? Probably I should; but to the end of my life I shall, in secret, hug and cherish this pathetic conceit. Yes, I shall hug and cherish it; for, let them say what they will, there is a certain thrilling sense of magical power that sometimes sweeps over me, as if from the shores of Lost Atlantis, promising things beyond the vision of hope.

Many people in England wonder at my love for America. Fools! How shall I ever pay back the debt I owe to this dear, mad, chaotic, scandalous country, where the women know "how to take care of themselves" and the men know how to take care of the women! No one with a tendency to love the great driving fatalistic rush of simplified elements, can help loving America.

Little things, little people, little distinctions, little niceties, little gardens, little houses, and little scandal,—how they are all swept aside and reduced to nothing in the torrent of this huge, grotesque, outrageous avalanche of human lava!

Things fall into their due proportion in America, into their true place under the Milky Way. "Culture" falls into its place, and the gentility of gentlemen, and the traditions and reverences of the past. How salutary, how refreshing, that immense nonchalant cynicism, that huge disregard for ceremony, that unrespect for persons!

For me, who find in England so much that obtrudes, that claims attention, that demands meticulous handling, what an escape, to be swept along on this tremendous torrent, where all separate things are *bleached*, as it were, into a common insignificance!

Individual objects and persons, those objects and persons that are so teasing and distracting in their emphatic colours, grow beautifully and monotonously *grey* as the winds of the great plains blow upon them. People grow to resemble one another and acquire a touching and profound modesty, a cosmic modesty, like that of sand-dunes or sea-pebbles, under the pressure of so vast a human tide.

I said, a little above, that I was no lover of humanity, and had small understanding of those who were. This is true. I am afraid the power of love is deplorably small in me. It is obvious that, if this be so, I myself am the worst sufferer from it. How strange it all is! One is born with certain faculties and qualities, or one is not. One is blamed or praised accordingly. But how unfair! Who of the children of men chose the womb that bore him?—who the orbits and transits of the stars under which he first saw the light?

But though not of amorous or loving temper, I am not always dull to the heart-breaking pathos of human life upon this earth. I think I feel it most, this melting mood, when, in a chance encounter on my journeys, the astounding gentleness and friendly consideration of some laborious child of toil hits me with a palpable hit of wonder. How can these victims of our social system remain so sweet-tempered, so courteous, so cordial? I know that all working people are not like that. I have met some as brutally, as boisterously arrogant, as any bloated slave-driver. But that there should be *any* so urbane, so sensitive, so tactful!—one is reconciled to the human race by such divine patience under such a lot.

To turn once more to the general attempt I am making to get at the bottom of those ideas and sensations which reveal my identity; I should not be true to my analytic conscience if I did not recognize one curious form of doubt which seems habitually present. I refer to the doubt as to whether what we call our "ideas" are really as important and prominent as we claim. What I seem to notice is that people are driven steadily forward by their inherited disposition and their circumstances; while the "ideas" that they project are only, as it were, little moving shadows and mirrored reflections of the inevitable stream of their destiny. It is appalling, the manner in which the mere outward conditions of our life mould, impress, and limit us. On the other hand, it is appalling how little the interchange of ideas and opinions affects our predestined, inherited temper.

My life, when I really examine it, turns out to be a perpetual series of bye-issues and interludes, under the surface of which my integral self waits and expects its free opportunity. Waits and expects it; and will be found waiting and expecting it, when my last hour strikes.

The real primitive, drastic elements in the drama are only these two. The underlying pressure of one's dominant will to enjoy, fettered and limited by the jagged and rough-edged obstacles of outward circumstances and conditions.

It is incredible,—the easy manner in which we conceal these facts, the hypocritical references and appeals we make to our moral sense and our philosophical ideas. The more what we esteem our virtue, is subjected to analysis, the more it turns out to be nothing but a rather sordid compromise between the exigencies of our insatiable, our corrupt will, and the hard sharp restraints of material conditions.

It is just this that gives me a feeling of shameful treachery to the facts of the case, when I advocate, in speaking and writing, my epicurean cult of elaborate and refined sensationalism. It would give a still worse feeling of shame if I launched out, as some do, into bold idealistic appeals to the supremacy of the spirit. In real life, how far does my epicurean cult actually affect my conduct? Not in the slightest degree. When circumstance throws me in the way of some object of attraction,—an exquisite field of flowers, an indescribable woodland solitude, an ancient city square or populous market-place, a sea-shore crowded with tender children, an enchanting group of fair youths or alluring maidens,—does my inner consciousness repeat to itself some liturgical formula about "our duty to make the most of every hour?" Not in the least. I just forget everything, and drink fiercely, desperately, of the cup of delectable vision. Suppose on the other hand, that some obtrusive diabolical necessity—a lecture to be given, an engagement to be fulfilled, a business transaction to be got through, an uncomfortable promise to be kept,—intervenes and summons me away, it is to no virtuous ethical principle that I submit, it is simply to the crude, unlovely pressure of brute circumstance.

IX

Some of my readers, if one finds readers for blunt, unvarnished indiscretions of this kind, will be perhaps wondering why, as I turn and turn about these pivotal points of my poor life's history, I say nothing of the "authors that have influenced me." Ah! for the very simple reason—the list would be too long! What portion of my being can be influenced by such things as books—and hopelessly bookish though I am, that portion is not very large—is influenced by every book I read.

As I have observed above, I think by books, I talk by books, I surround everything that occurs to me by a bookish atmosphere. Books make a fine, mellow, imaginative mist, through which I see things and people thrown to an enchanting distance. Yes, I think by books. But, here again, when it comes to the point, I do not live by books.

For instance, because books upon Greek Art assure me that the exquisite limbs of boys and girls are more important objects of contemplation, and more revealing of the Platonic ideal of Beauty, than trees and flowers, I do not therefore leave my solitary valley in the Sussex Downs, and rush to the beach at Brighton. Or when the mood is on me and I sit enraptured by the airy movements of a Pavlowa or an Isadora Duncan, I do not tear myself away and retreat to the wilderness because, in the intervals of the acts, I glance over some mystic Wordsworthian sonnet, or some verse from the Prophet Isaiah.

I do not doubt my friends because Emerson recommends "living to oneself." I do not shun the society of gentle ladies because Schopenhauer says unkind things about the shape of their figures.

The influence which books have over me, is like the influence of some constant orchestral accompaniment. One moves from group to group, as the band plays; but the music does not the least modify one's inveterate tastes and proclivities. It heightens one's pleasure here; it softens one's disappointment there. It is the atmosphere of one's life-drama; but over the material sequence of acts and scenes, it has no power at all.

Of course my inborn disposition largely *affects* my taste in books. My absolute indifference to artistic form, and my passion for analytical suggestion, obviously lead me to prefer *Jean Christophe* to *Madame Bovary;* and *Crime and Punishment* to a short story by *De Maupassant.* I have the power also—a rare power it seems, judging from the grotesque misunderstandings of the official critics—of taking my favourite authors with a pinch of salt. I am able, for instance, to appreciate Nietzsche's slashing onslaughts upon the gregarious tyranny of weakness, without any obsequious veneration for the blond assassin.

My rôle in the lecturing field seems naturally to assume the character of an attempt to instill a little imagination into the public's mind. I love Nietzsche's pulverizing insight and his noble and aristocratic tone; but I do not feel in the least bound to accept as infallible oracles his portentous utterances about Eternal Recurrence and the Higher Morality. The former theory seems based on very doubtful premises, and the latter demands an austere nobility of nature which is far out of my reach.

Simple and naive indeed are those easy pagan souls who dream that this devastating sage's haughty imperatives will be found kinder to their pleasant vices than the rules of the Church. The Higher Morality may condone what we poor Pantagruelian Christians have been taught to regard as crime; but the glacial airs of its mountainous summits will freeze with intolerable disdain our little earthy frailties.

When one demands a real magnetic clairvoyance in regard to the subtler things, when one cries out for a full interpretive understanding of the world-thick volume of human fatality, its treacherous undercurrents, its subterranean perversities, it is not, I think so much to Nietzsche's flashing northern lights that one turns, as to the less arbitrary revelations of a Dostoevsky or a Henry James.

But—to revert to my bewildering contradictions—it is a most curious psychological spectacle to watch the widening gulf between one's dramatic imagination of what a human life upon earth ought to be, and the real, actual thing that one's life has in practice become.

In writing of myself I am tempted, for instance, to make much of the effect upon my mind of sudden little changes in my surroundings. I like to speak of myself as being affected by those whispers and rumours, those signs and signals, which come and go so magically and wantonly about the paths of us all. The sudden falling of a cool shadow across a dusty road; the flicker of yellow sunlight through the doorway of some wayside barn; the gleam of a sea-gull's wings in the track of a great ship; the mystery of a solitary bridge or river-weir, heavy with the mutterings of the wind and water; the look of some lonely poplar tree where nothing but marsh-reeds and grey mists can see its absorption into the Night;—these chance hieroglyphics of the Moving Finger should be, according to my imagination of my wayfaring, turning-points and conversions of deep spiritual significance. But they are nothing of the kind. I see them, I note them, I avariciously appropriate to myself their evasive charm. But that is all. It ends there. They do not penetrate the opaque material substance of my real identity.

It is a sad confession to have to make, but the truth is I have grown cynically "endued unto the element" of my habitual temper; and my habitual temper allows for no sudden and thrilling revelations. Those wonderful second-thoughts and earth-escaping ecstasies, which I am able to describe only too eloquently in words, never come to me in life. "I see, not feel," how significant these omens are. I peer up at Arcturus and Orion: but these celestial travellers do not throb and vibrate for me with divine reassurances. All those miraculous intimations which the poets draw, from the moaning of forest-branches and the shadows in moon-lit lakes, leave me untouched and unmoved in my earth-bound proclivity. And yet I am not dull to their appeal. My senses are not atrophied. I do not pass by these magical significations with philistine indifference. It is only that a certain heavy, cynical, fatalistic doubt as to the possibility of their having any real message for me, paralyzes my spiritual response.

My analytic mind is always at hand, ready to reduce to physiological causes every stir and lift of the emotional soul.

It may be true in spite of what I have said earlier in these pages, that I really have anarchistic longings for something surprising, uncaused, arbitrary and chaotic, in the stream of things: as I grow older, these wayward cravings diminish, and I tend to give myself up more and more completely to a vision of the world that is limited, categorical, and determined.

This leads me to a further problem in the analysis of my disposition. It is queer to note how active and insatiable my *mind* is, as compared with the paralysis of my *spirit*. I fancy that pride has something to do with this. I seem to have inherited pride of intellect combined with contempt for spiritual susceptibility. I am always tempted to accuse spiritually sensitive people of hypocrisy, affectation, and self-deception. I suspect them of false interpretations of purely physiological feelings.

My dislike of spiritual emotion is further enhanced by a cautious dread I have of being fooled by the Universe. It is odd that I should have this peculiarity; for I rather like, as I have hinted, feeling and being a fool in the opinion of humanity. It is one of my little ways of being revenged upon people—this tendency to make faces and act like a lunatic in their presence. But though I like being a fool before men, I do not like being a fool before Nature. I am extremely reluctant to concede to this great sarcastic Parent which brought me forth, the power to drug me with its insidious drugs. When I read what the shrewd old Goethe says about not destroying the essential Illusions, I feel a grim satisfaction in noting that that sly world-child knew well enough that they *were* Illusions.

It is important here that I should emphatically protest that my dislike of spiritual ecstasies has nothing to do with .the infirmity of my flesh. One's mental moods are undoubtedly enormously influenced by one's physical moods; and my physical moods are often extremely devastating.

I suffer from chronic gastric weakness. An inherited tendency to gastric ulceration, nervous dyspepsia, and inflation of the stomach, hangs, like a constant cloud of deadly vapour, over my activities. I am driven to a thousand hypochondriacal precautions and avoidances. My diet is an invalid's diet, my nerves are an invalid's nerves. Ulcers are not cheerful companions for an Epicure's path through life.

The stomach is the concentration-point for every one of our most thrilling reactions. It is in the pit of the stomach that one feels the ache of nostalgia and the ache of desire, as well as the ache of indigestion. Undoubtedly my aesthetic appreciation of many charming things is blurred and clouded by this infirmity. Its yoke is exhausting and I make no doubt that much of my tired inclination for the liberating poppies of Proserpine are due to its burden.

It is difficult to idealize the stomach. It is not an agreeable thought that one's end, when it does come, will probably be due to some unlovely fungoid growth at the centre of one's nervous sensibilities. One would sooner be eaten by silvery fishes than by a gross leaden coloured polypus.

I wonder if the reader of this little sketch has yet divined a certain aspect of my character which I have myself only recently recognized? A person might suppose, from the tone I sometimes adopt, that I live an epicurean life of meticulously self-conscious sensations, passing from one to another with an inward unction of avaricious concentration. I do nothing of the kind. It would be impossible to find a human being with a less firm hold upon the stream of his emotional experiences. My consciousness is hardly ever turned inward: my experiences are hardly ever gathered up into a deliberate or definite continuity. I plunge from attraction to attraction, from lure to lure from obsession to obsession, with the simple unpremeditated greediness of a child. I never survey myself with detached and intelligent interest. I never organize or mould myself. I never contemplate myself with tender or humorous pity. In this sense I have none of the sentimentalist in me. I have nothing of the artist either. I do not search about for my most characteristic vision of the world, and then deliberately fortify it and emphasize it with laborious effort.

Those among my friends who possess the sharp edges of the artist's mind are irritated and provoked by the drifting and chaotic manner in which my sensations succeed one another with no symbolic orientation. To *cultivate* my senses, on the lines of an imaginative and individual vision, is an impossibility to me. It is not an impossibility because of indolence, as some have thought. I am not an indolent person; I am a restlessly active one. It is an impossibility because I am unwilling to sacrifice any one single sensual pleasure to another. And it is only out of sacrifice of this kind that the true artist's vision is banked up and protected from dissolution.

I have no imaginative perseverance, no aesthetic method. I clutch at one thing after another with infantile absorption. In doing so I absolutely forget myself. My consciousness is entirely taken up with the outward thing that draws me. This is quite the contrary of the artist's way. Artists never forget themselves. They use outward things only as mirrors and musical stops, by which they see their own image and hear their own voice heightened and enlarged. Another cause of my inability to cultivate the artist's vision is my inveterate scepticism. I am sceptical about the truth of every phase of refinement in these hyper-sensitive explorations. This is of course an absurd obstacle, because objective truth has nothing to do with the artist's imagination. He has a perfect right to treat it with contempt; and, out of a scepticism quite as deep as mine, to create a world of original reality entirely his own.

I cannot do this, and I find myself irresistibly led to regard as unnatural, conceited, affected, and silly, those who achieve it. When I meet such patient creators of their own elaborate vision, I feel tempted to jeer and jibe at them from a point of view as grossly philistine as that of any ignorant country boor.

And yet, even as I write these words— O the subtle hiding-places of vanity!— I am, in my heart of hearts, conscious of a sort of self-satisfied pride that I regard these people as affected and insincere. Is it a queer vein of Puritanism in me, or a vein of rough bucolic humour, that produces this complacency? But, no! Away with such mock-modesty! What I really feel is that, in my blundering chaotic way, I am nearer to the great fermenting vats of the elemental world than these curled darlings of wilful fancy. It is, I suppose, this rude earthy realism in my composition that makes it so hard for me to appreciate the elaborate overtones and rhythmic suggestions of the Futurist and Cubist schools of painting.

Post-Impressionism, on the contrary, I love and admire; and hold it a great and invaluable experiment in the history of Art. This is because Post-Impressionism has a fine barbaric sense of the splendid magic of the surface of things—that surface of things where I habitually live; whereas those others go digging away at what to me are profoundly uninteresting "Mathematical Harmonies" of a very doubtful "World-Beneath."

As to what is called Free Verse, I am quite friendly to it, as long as it deals, in realistic bitterness and earthly tang, with the old essential ironies and insults of Fate's common ways with her mortal children. It is when it launches out into mystical abstruseness, and recondite occultism, into symbolic mythology and images drawn from fairy-land, that I detest and despise it.

Free Verse apart, what really appeals to me in poetry is the high penetrating beauty of great magical single lines: such lines as one comes across in Horace and Milton and Dante. And I notice that these lines invariably have to do with the noble suggestiveness of the surface of things—the surface of things as it has always been.

X

IN REGARD to my feelings for my friends —
I love *genius* above everything.   The
appearance of genius, even in a person
otherwise intolerable, makes me always tender and considerate.   The hesitations and
timidities and aberrations of a person of weak
will possessed of genius, fill me with tactful
regard.   On the contrary, towards strong-
willed persons of vigorous but unimaginative
intellect, my attitude is sometimes quite
unkind.   At the same time I observe as an
interesting physiological fact, that the society of nervous and ill-constituted people
throws me, inwardly, into a reaction of hard,
clear, and even philistine capacity.   Below
the surface, though I trust I show no sign
of this, I become sharp, definite, resolute,
aggressive and practical.   Imaginative
people of a nebulous incoherence, tend to
throw me by reaction into a tightly-strung
mood of energetic cleverness.

I think I am, as a matter of fact, rather
clever than otherwise; only my suscepti-

bility to sensual obsessions clouds and drugs my cleverness. I am indeed much cleverer than my enemies suppose; though this does not give my pride much satisfaction, for what I admire in my heart is genius, and genius alone.

I am so clever that, in the intellectual sphere, it is not easy to fool me; whereas I notice that people of genius are constantly being fooled. They are indeed of a pathetic simplicity. I am not simple; though the naive manner in which I pursue my sensations, sometimes gives that impression. I am inclined to assert, though it seems an amazing claim to make, that my habitual attitude towards people, even towards the people I love the best, is one of Machiavellian dissimulation. Of course this may be nothing but a pathetic illusion. It is quite possible that my friends see through me without the slightest difficulty, and that my self-satisfied diplomacy appears to them the most naive childishness. Perhaps it is even a constant joke among them at my expense. I have an inkling that I have discerned already something of this kind, especially in regard to my admiration for their artistic achievements. I have begun to suspect that they have got weary of my perpetual habit of agreement and unqualified assent. This suspicion has led me recently into the application of certain jolts and shocks, the success of which, in exciting my friends' respect, has induced me to question the wisdom of my cunning. There is no doubt I must have gone a good deal too far upon this path of universal acquiescence. It has led me into certain very grotesque situations, due indirectly to its annihilation of my friends' respect for me, as a formidable fellow who might "hit back."

I suppose I have cultivated an absurd idea that one's friends respect one and treat one considerately, in proportion as one refrains from self-assertion. Nothing could be more untrue. One's friends' respect is secured and sustained precisely in the same manner as is one's enemies'; that is to say by the imposition upon them of the formidableness of power. Quite apart from Machiavellian diplomacy, I have, by disposition, an extreme reluctance to assert my will against another's will. It gives me pleasure to pillory myself, to humiliate myself, to appear as a clumsy clown, a

doddering fool, an apologetic and character-
less nincompoop, in the presence of those
who are really fond of me.

From the results of this proclivity upon
the minds of my friends, I have learned
the interesting fact that even in friendship
one has to make oneself feared in order to
be treated considerately and on equal terms.
In a sense what I am now saying is unfair
to my friends; and for this reason: when a
person shows that he derives a certain perverse pleasure from being roughly used, it
is difficult to resist the temptation to use
him roughly. Nor is it with me only a
matter of the pleasure of being thus scolded
and criticised. In addition to this voluptuous perversity there is present in the depths
of my heart a certain malicious delight in
leading my critics on, so that they may be
more and more betrayed and inveigled in
the damning quagmire of moral complacency. The more unjust their strictures are,
the further they betray themselves; and I
am sometimes guilty of even playing up
to their false accusations in order that they
may arrive at a quite ridiculous pass. Such
a pass, for instance, as they are brought to,
when their flagrant over-riding strikes the

astonished attention of some mutual acquaintance, who regards their ardour as pure insanity. In the estimation of this third person I appear as a mild, harmless, and even saintly individual, outrageously persecuted. It is only when this poor triumph begins to grow tedious, that I sarcastically divest myself of my champion and rush back to my purgatorial circle on the wings of fierce repentance.

It is very interesting to note how, in such a word-juggler as I am, the instincts of the artist should be so thin. When I write a book, I never write for posterity, or for the love of rounding off an exquisite and finished work. I write to give a certain malicious prod to my enemies, and a certain thrilling caress to my friends. I write with quite definite people always before me, who will be amused or irritated in a quite definite manner. This is the case with my lecturing. The general public is never anything to me. It simply does not exist. The idea of making it cry or laugh, the idea of converting it to this or that, never enters my head. I am either a special pleader "in vacuo" for some favourite author, or I am addressing a quite personal appeal to some single member of the audience. I am, in fact, either making love to some noble antique spirit, or I am cajoling and propitiating some evasive modern bearer of enchantments. The real physiological history of my "art of lecturing" would be a strange page of mental revelation. I must confess that it often seems to me as though I were swept away, out of my own methods and consciousness, on the tide of some invisible force. The "general public," as I have said, have never any existence for me. But sometimes the obsession grows deeper. My own personal motives are transcended, I forget my occasion, my author, and my friends, and am driven on from utterance to utterance, like a man speaking under the influence of some drug or hypnotic suggestion.

Many explanations, but none quite satisfactory, occur to me as the solution of this phenomenon. Some would say that I have the power, under given conditions, of drawing upon what certain psychologists call the subliminal consciousness and that the inspiration of this consciousness, flowing from a source more general and impersonal than the individual brain of one speaker, shows a clairvoyance and an energy beyond what it would be possible for me to reach in any normal moods. My own view of the case is not quite this. I dislike having recourse to these pseudo-supernatural explanations. I fancy that a certain type of speaker possessed of abnormal sensitiveness to mental vibrations, can become as it were intoxicated by the minds of his hearers, and, without being the least conscious of it, be mesmerized into certain inspirations of insight, quite unattainable by him when alone and in cold blood.

It may be said that there is not much difference between these explanations. There is at least this difference, that the latter accounts for these impersonal outbursts without having recourse to any hypothesis of a subliminal "soul of the world," independent of particular individuals.

I said, earlier in this sketch, that my controlling object of life and the chief aim of my activity was Pleasure and Pleasure alone. Am I led to announce this out of my hatred of Moralists and Idealists, or is this a real dominant motive with me?

O! how hard it is to analyze with true exactness one's motives and feelings in these dubious borderlands! And if there is such a vein of malicious provocation in what I utter, why is it that I should have such vindictive spleen against a set of worthy, if not very profound, fellow-mortals?

Let me do with this latter point first. I think I get to the root of the matter when I say that my hatred of Moralists does not spring from any antinomian fear lest they should interfere with me personally. My personal aberrations are not of the kind they could interfere with. It is rather that they interfere with my interest in life in general, and with my appreciation of the Universe. What, in my fatalistic way, I like to see and feel and touch, are those powerful direct emotions, which men and animals, and even plants, experience, when the life-lust pushes them forward between the hot sun and the thick earth, to wrestle, and play, and bask, and expand, and breathe freely, and stretch forth tongues and horns, and snouts, and hands, and tails.

I like to know that on a Sunday after-noon, in even the quietest village, lads and wenches are making unceremonious love to each other in the shady lanes. I like to know that tramps are stealing chickens, children bursting through hedges, maidens plotting to run away from their parents, farmers laying schemes to outwit landlords, labourers conspiring together to plunder farmers, and the Lord of the Manor setting gentlemanly gins to waylay the feet of the clergyman. It does not even distress me to think of the clergyman himself, that Pillar of Morality, snatching a forbidden embrace from his amorous kitchen wench under the kindly privet hedge. Think, my noble Theophilus, how little of a dramatic picture would be left for your ironic soul if these natural outbursts of primitive passion were trimmed and pruned into submission?

But to return to the matter of Pleasure. Let me suppose that my stark statement—that I follow no other end than this—be no mere piece of reactionary spleen hurled at the head of Moralists. Is it a true and exact account of what I am? Do I really and truly make Pleasure my single aim? O! the difficulty and ambiguity of these questions! It annoys me to admit it, because of my queer, inverted craving for making myself out as frivolous as possible; but I suppose the truth is that my pursuit of Pleasure is a very indirect and complicated affair. I am really blundering absurdly in the confusion of words. As a matter of fact, I daily sacrifice the pleasure of the senses to the pleasure of the mind. I sacrifice the pleasure of direct sensation to the pleasure of power, and the pleasure of power to the pleasure of being affectionately loved. I sacrifice the pleasure of thrilling excitement to the pleasure of thrilling quietness, and the pleasure of voluptuous pursuit to the pleasure of philosophical conversation.

Yes, it is only, after all, in a very qualified sense that I am that intransigeant Hedonist I should like my moralistic friends to find me. But there is something in my claim. I do respond more quickly and spontaneously than many to the immediate sensational appeal. I live more in the present hour than most people; and am more easily swept out of my calculated temper by the lures of the occasion. The moment governs me more absorbingly than it seems to govern others, and I am more a slave of the immediate attraction of a chance encounter. This unbalanced and chaotic following of the will-o'-wisps of accidental beckonings, is partly due to the fact that my tired scepticism is always muttering to me in a low plaintive voice, and nudging me on, to be inconsistent and inconsequent. "All is equal," it keeps repeating; "all is equal; and nothing matters."

I sometimes wonder if I am regarded by my friends and acquaintances as a *reliable* person—as a person to whom they would turn, in an emergency, for help and support. If not, this were a grave blow to my self-esteem. I should like to be the kind of person people would regard as absolutely reliable and dependable. "He is an egoist, of course," I should like them to say, "but one can always depend upon him at a pinch."

Will the friends of my heart, that I have, in one kind and another, so sorely abused, ever forgive me, and have confidence in me again? I would have you believe, O grievously tried companions, that beyond the thick marshmists of my imperviousness I am constantly hoisting signals and lighting beacon-fires. I would have you think of me not as some insolent despiser of human affection, not as some brazen image of impervious self-contentment; but as one who knows only too well what he lacks of spiritual fire, of one who can at least visualize the wretched gap in his nature where the "soul" and its tender attributes ought to be.

I do not stiffen myself in any obdurate in-sensitiveness. I bow to the fatality that has made me what I am; but I worship also, at the outer gate of the sanctuary of high devotion, the beautiful gods of renunciation and remorse.

I cannot help referring, once more, while I am upon this subject, to the effect of the present war upon my mind. I wonder what would be the impression upon me if my health, my youth, and my courage lent themselves to such a thing as a few weeks in the trenches?

My attitude to the war is by no means that of some pacific and philosophical friends of my acquaintance. I regard all the young men who go, and the middle-aged men still more, as genuine heroes. I admire them; I respect them; I feel a certain shame in their presence. The mere neigh-bourhood of these terrific struggles has the effect of reducing the personal importance of all my thoughts and feelings to a minimum of interest. It does not so much give me the feeling of the importance of our cause against that of the enemy, as of the trifling and ephemeral nature of all causes, in the presence of these great catastrophic outbursts of nature's malignity. I have not the remotest sympathy with those sleek and secure philosophers who speak of the benefits of war. I have more intelligence than that. Those who go to war are worthy of all admiration; but what waste—what incredible waste! I think, though it may give my ethical friends more pleasure than I like to give them, that the effect of a few weeks in the trenches would be to make me resolve to spend the rest of my life writing desperately and savagely against time,— writing everything I have it in me to write, —writing ferociously with hardly a breathing-space. I note that even at this safe distance the effect of these huge naval and military struggles has been to keep me more closely at my work. I have written more laboriously, more carefully, in this last year, than ever before in my life. What does this mean? I suppose it means that my inherited race-conscience, pricked and roused in me by the presence of heroic fortitude in another field, does what it can to free itself from its burden by an increased laboriousness in the sphere of its normal activity.

Should I have the moral courage, I wonder, to admire as a philosophical *tour-de-force*, the attitude of a person absolutely unaffected in his personal conscience by the war; of a person who continued his way, as imperviously untouched as the seagulls in the Dardanelles, or the wild-fowl on the Flemish marshes? Whether I should admire such a person, or shrink from him in moral astonishment, I do not know. I only know that for myself I have nothing of this god-like equanimity.

XI

To leave the war-question, and revert
once more to my general philosophical
attitude. The reader will remember
that I referred at the beginning of this sketch
to my feeling that the universe was at once
determined by inexorable laws and liable to
irrational surprises. I said that I "wished"
the Universe to be framed in this fashion,
in order that it might preserve at the same
time its unassailable fatality and its inexplicable mystery. I do not repent of
using in regard to these high philosophical
speculations the word "wish" with all its
presumptuous personal implications. If I
am convinced of anything in this world, I
am convinced of the presence, in every
philosophical system, of the original wish,
or will, or temperamental bias, of the individual philosophizing. What does trouble
me is the thought that, even in what I
have said, there may remain an element of
word-mongering. It is so difficult to divest
oneself of the associations of words, and to

use them freshly and spontaneously as real symbols. What one would like to do, would be to use words not so much as the vehicle of thought, as of direct physical sensation; but this is an enterprise that requires more genius than I possess.

I am so afraid lest, even in what I have tried to say about my feeling of the pressure of Fate, I should have been led into wordy exaggeration. I do not, however, think that I can possibly exaggerate the constant presence with me of a steady invincible mechanic force, pushing me forward from point to point, from stage to stage, and giving me no loophole of escape. In calling this thing by the old classical name of Fate, I must not be supposed to be personifying it. I do not think of it in the remotest degree as conscious, still less as benign. I think of it as absolutely beyond our analysis. And if I try to analyze its effect upon myself, I can only say that I feel there is relief in submitting to it, and misery in struggling against it.

I suppose no one is more addicted than myself to becoming the infatuated slave of attractive word-combinations. My abnormal and insatiable receptivity—a sort of

sensual voluptuousness in the intellectual
world—makes me especially liable to attach
too great value to these fashionable catch-
words. My pliable and serpentine cleverness leads me to wind myself into every
new word-edifice with slippery agility. A
certain power of rapid and logical assimu-
lation tempts me to pass off as my own con-
clusions views and visions which are really
quite alien to myself. My scepticism en-
courages this fault by constantly reminding
me that anything may be true, and that I
may as well select one view of things as any
other. I have what I suppose is a Latin
mind in these matters; and I find myself
continually tempted to give that curious
complexion of logical-imaginative plausi-
bility, wherein French writers are so cunning,
to points of view quite foreign to my own
nature. All this is obviously the sort of
intellectual quicksand into which the profession of a lecturer would naturally betray
a man.

And yet it is absurd to blame my profession. The fault is my own, and the inevitable defect of my critical and sceptical
quality. The same defect may be observed
in my style of writing; though here there

are undoubtedly weighty compensations. I have, in fact, unless it be impossible to catch the flavour of one's own manner, *no* style at all. My writing is as transparent and clear, as colourless and fluid, as my mind. I fear that it is the style of every ordinarily intelligent person who "reads the recent writers." If so, all I can do is to try and make it the vehicle for a certain drastic sincerity which is certainly not yet the attribute of the ordinarily intelligent person. I can myself see, as I read my own writing, how difficult it is for me to substitute for all these clumsy pseudo-scientific words, with which one's books burden one, the kind of suggestive natural imagery, touched with delicate perfumes and light-blowing airs, which gives so gracious a body to analytic thought.

There is however a certain intellectual pleasure to be derived from the mere contemplation of a sincere writer's wrestling with an evasive subject, even though his style does remain awkward and bare; and it is with this pleasure that my readers must be contented.

I cannot think that, in this matter of my consciousness of Fatality, I am being fooled by my love of words, as I was when I used to protest my devotion to Chaos and Chance. In that case, I certainly did, in my nimble and clever way, snatch fervently at what was an intellectual fashion. This Chaos-cult was further encouraged in me by the influence of certain among my friends; particularly he of the iron hand in the velvet glove, whose present pastorage is beyond the Equator, and he of the titanic spirit in the humorous mask, whose habitation is with the herds of Manhattan. Both these original spirits are addicted to speaking as if this steady, forward-driving world, as it appears to me, were tossed from side to side, and upheaved, and shaken, and blown about, and swept by strange storms and tornadoes belched forth from elemental abysses. The honest truth is that I do not feel these wayward incursions, these arbitrary explosions. What I feel is the slow majestic march forward of the planetary hosts with all their offspring; and the steady uninterrupted thud-thud-thud of the great fatal Engines of Inexorable Law.

I can remember, years ago, in Chicago, arguing fiercely with that inspired Idealist, the Manager of the Little Theatre there, on this very subject. He held the view, as I do now, that the world is governed by irreversible Necessity—only to him this Necessity appeared a thing of mystical benignity, beautiful and sublime. I argued, savagely enough, in favour of absolute cosmic anarchy. I am inclined to think, at this distance, that I was pushed into this absurd position by my rage at the idea of a benignant order. I did not see then, as I see now, that it is quite possible to have an order from which there is no escape, without its being in the least benignant.

Will my reader be able to keep his temper if I go yet one step farther in this re-consideration, in this analysis of an analysis? I plead guilty, hurriedly and without remorse, to the charge of ridiculous inconsistency in these discoveries. I am digging and digging into my profoundest feelings, and instead of throwing away the alien weeds that grow on the top of the soil, I pile them up as interesting specimens, side by side with roots and rock-chippings of much more deeply buried things. It is just here I may remark that I differ in opinion from my excellent relative, the

Hermit of Egdon. His view seems to be that the deeper you dig into human nature, the more chaotic and startling are your discoveries. In talking with him, I always feel as though below the surface of every human being, lurked a great howling gorilla of ungovernable ferocity.

My feeling is exactly the contrary, and does not at all, when I really probe into the matter, suggest these hidden Calibans. What I feel is that the erratic things, the snarling, irrational things, are all on the surface; and as soon as you get below the surface, you touch the vast granite slabs of the huge Mill-Wheel of irreversible, inevitable Order.

I am sure this impression of mine is supported by my experience of my own character. It is on the surface that I hate people and long to revenge myself on people. In the depths of myself, I neither love them nor hate them: I am part of the Eternal Mechanism, and my arrogant heart is no more than a small clock-work fragment of the great Time-piece of everlasting Necessity. I do not for a moment agree with this desperate view of the profound wickedness of human nature. I do not

find human nature either wicked or good.
I find it driven forward by the same inevitable laws as the tides and the con-
stellations.

Shall I confess to my reader how my own
most inveterate vices appear to me? They
appear to me as irritable mouths and
tongues and fingers, itching and vibrating,
on the most outward surface of my being.
They appear to me as insatiable superficial
nerves of my bodily texture—connected
indeed, by tiny invisible threads, with the
cells of my brain, but always ready, if they
are drugged with satisfaction, to sink into a
state of indifferent quiescence. To turn
one's little bodily insanities into these great
Leviathans of the Deep, seems to me to
evince a lamentable lack of mental proportion. It is an affair of the surface—an
affair of nerves and sensory vibrations.

What I am led more and more to feel is
that, however desperate and deep our
anti-social desires may seem, and however
passionate and exalted our ethical ideals
may seem, they are neither of them, in the
great cosmic system, of the least importance.
They come and they go, both our evil
impulses and our noble impulses; and it

matters little how they succeed one another. What matters, if anything matters, is something subtler, more wonderful, than either what we call good or what we call evil; something that has no name because it has not reached the rational level which enables it to be put into words; but something all the same which is the very secret of existence. Perhaps it is this that I approach when I get such strange satisfaction from "lying back" upon eternal Destiny —that Destiny which is neither benignant nor malign. "But why not benignant?" my reader may exclaim. Well! there we touch again that inveterate prejudice I feel against a world ruled by Providence. If I could get to the bottom of this prejudice, I should indeed get to the bottom of myself. Earlier in this sketch I endeavoured to defend this bias on purely aesthetic grounds. Was I justified in so doing? Burrowing round and round this pivotal problem, in my dogged, tiresome, persistent manner, I am tempted to ask myself the question whether this prejudice against an invisible Guiding Hand is not merely one of those superficial nervous vices to which I have above referred. Do I quarrel with the idea of Providence merely out of itching, sensory irritation, which I feel sometimes towards my most attractive neighbour? Is it simply the surliness of the material-minded animal, drawing back and snarling, at the approach of the amiable stranger?

No! I do not believe it! The thing goes deeper than that; deeper perhaps even than the aesthetic question. There is something in me—and it is no mere superficial perversity—which demands an element of cold, unconscious, sublime fatality in the texture of things.

Human love is exquisite and rare. It is desirable, as all delicate things that are short-lived and easily destroyed are desirable. But there are other things than love in this huge world. I am not thinking now of malice, or vindictiveness, or violence. These are only the reverse side of love, and are its inevitable accompaniment. I am thinking of great, cool, large, magical, ordered Spaces, where the winds of eternal Necessity blow without interruption, and where nothing can ever come that is warm, conscious, friendly, human.

Yes; down in the depths of my being lurks, like a physical craving for air, a longing for vast, uninhabited, untraversed regions, where even God never comes. I cannot help it. This is the manner in which I am made. I long to escape from humanity, to escape from myself; and how can I do so if the centre and circumference of the world are the habitation of a God who embraced humanity, and is anxious to embrace me?

It is precisely this anarchical rebelliousness in my spirit that makes me feel such a thrill of sympathy with Goethe's Mephistopheles, when that queer Child of Chaos expresses his wish that this "All" had never originally issued from that "Nothing." So here, it appears, we really do touch the bottom; and this perpetual harping upon abnormal feelings, proves to be the result not of a longing for arbitrary explosions of wayward life-forces, but of a longing for quietness and rest,—for cool, deep, eternal, Godless night.

With this clue in my hand it becomes easier for me to thread the labyrinth of my disposition. I ought to be able, with its help to compel even my style to flow

nonchalantly, more smoothly, more naturally; and cease its fumbling after fashionable
catch-words. To escape from myself, to escape from humanity, to escape from everything that obtrudes and challenges and ex-
acts, and is attracted and repulsed,—such is
the secret of my hidden craving. This is why
the moon appeals to me. In moonlight,
things are softened, and rendered liquid and
flowing. Every separate object loses its
garish individuality, and seems to float
free on a cool, luminous tide of self-effacement. The windless expanses of the ocean
have the same effect; and nothing is more
beautiful to me than to see islands and
promontories, capes and headlands, swim-
ming in a delicate, transfiguring mist of
motionless water.

It is when the moon rises over wide
stretches of level sand at the sea's edge,
that one can most easily sink away, out of
the body of one's prison, into the large
magical horizons where the weariness of
thought is purged, and the heart is at peace.

> "For the sword outwears its sheath,
> And the soul outwears the breast;
> And the heart must pause to breathe;
> And love itself have rest."

My friends have often laughed at me for this fantastic devotion to the moon; and rallied me for my sudden indifference to their conversation when the translunar magic has rapt me away, down long quivering, silvery paths, out of the reach of both hate and love; but I have not felt remorse. They have pointed out how inconsistent such devotion is with my nervous, almost feline dislike of damp grass and dewy fields; and so it may be. Certainly the feeling of dampness in the air—the approach of rain, the rising of the wind—always dispel these fragile emotions. A touch of chilliness, of cold physical discomfort, is sufficient to drive me back, miserable and disenchanted, into my human cave. That is why my ideal of happiness would be to sit under the shadow of some Desert Temple, in a hot southern night, and watch the moon mount up, lovely and contemptuous, above the palm-trees.

But the sun himself has the same power; especially when in his heavy noons he bleaches the grass, bakes the sand, and burns the dust.

Further, as I have suggested above, certain cities of men evoke, in their various ways, this oblivious monotony. Venice does it by the elimination of street-noises; London by the obliterating power of her immensity and her mists; New York by the engine-driven uniformity of her tremendous traffic.

Life is so constructed, that, out of our most lamentable weakness, Nature creates the quality in us which is our genius and our triumph. My greatest weakness is this profound weariness of the struggle,—this withdrawing from the creative stream, —this sinking back into the monotony of the unruffled face of the waters. And yet this very self-effacement is an initiation and an enlargement; for where I merge myself in the spaces and the elements, I obtain something of their eternity and their calm. What is perturbed and agitated in me sinks into the gulf; and my essential being, given over to the waveless, windless, forward-sweeping tide of what flows and flows forever, becomes part and parcel of that eternal stuff which cannot change or be increased or diminished,—the stuff out of which all the dreams of life are made, and into which they all must sink at the end.

Let there be no misunderstanding about this. I am not in the smallest degree what people call a "mystic quietist." My sceptical detachment from all I do and say, and from what all others do and say, has nothing in it of a secret lying back upon hidden spiritual forces, which are the true reality. I do not believe in such forces. I do not believe in such a reality.

If ever I experience the sensation that all we little men and women are muttering to one another in dreams and making meaningless gestures over a vast gulf, it is not that I feel the reality of things to be flowing below us all the while, strange and rich and wonderful; it is that I feel the projections and excrescences, the protrusions and assertions, to be vain and futile, while the great smooth marble-faced Wheels of Fate turn inexorably on their axles.

This is why in ordinary conversation I am so often *distrait* and absent-minded, or am so ready with a languid assent. I seem to have heard the same thing said over and over again a million times. I watch in my friends the inevitable working of the machinery that makes them just thus and not otherwise. I hear the "tick-

tick-tick" of the everlasting clock-work behind them. I know too well, long before their sentences are finished, what those sentences are going to be.

Knowing them—poor galvanic microcosms of the great Necessity—and knowing the limits of their destined reactions, why should I be so interested in watching their little jerks and spasms and grindings? I know well the sound of the pitiful creak of the machinery that started them, and I know well the pitiful sound of the click with which they will run down.

In every situation that occurs I see the wires vibrating that will break it up. Why should I lend myself to the great Illusion by uttering earnest and emphatic words about my opinions and my convictions, or by trying to express to people my philosophy? This is one of the reasons which make me so unsatisfactory a companion. Everybody else has the power of getting excited in what is called "argument." I cannot get excited and angry in argument. I find it extremely difficult to get angry at all. To get angry implies that you believe in free-will,—in the freedom of people to be different from what they are, and to say different things. I do not believe in such freedom. I know beforehand exactly what people are going to say. What can I do then but listen, and nod my head, and mutter "Really!" and "Fancy that!" and "How interesting!"

It is for this reason that when I do assert myself and get excited, it is always about some absurd little physical thing which touches one of my tastes or distastes. I can grow eloquent and utter very vehement words about my preference for blue over yellow, or for satin over velvet, or for horse-hair sofas over cushioned couches. I can use very plausible speech with people when my window does not open, or my fire does not burn, or my pen does not write. But to spend breath upon them because they are Anglicans, or Free-Lovers, or Mormons, or Necrophiliasts, seems to me mere weariness of the flesh.

The whole of what we call social intercourse—when there is nothing sexual in it—is based upon this kind of illusion. I have never been able to derive the least pleasure either from "light conversation" or "intellectual disputes." Wit and persiflage bore me, as they say, "to extinction."

I only "shine" in conversation when I am allowed to discourse upon my physical sensations or upon my aesthetic tastes. The art of conversation is an odious nuisance to me,—as disagreeable as cards;—and how any intelligent person can prefer it to reading a book, or indulging in a flirtation, I cannot conceive.

It is this terrible and constant response to the "thud-thud-thud" of the great universal Engines, which makes me throw myself so fiercely into the few distractions that do dull my intelligence. When some provoking butterfly-lure beckons me over hill and dale, it is something if the excitement of the pursuit prevents my perverted mind from hearing the throbs of that hope-murdering World-Pump.

It is perhaps one of those stupid blunders into which I am myself always falling, when I talk of the direct connection between my bodily wishes and my rational mind. In reality my mind, as compared with the minds of other people of tolerable cleverness, seems remarkably independent of my body. It is independent of my imagination, of my artistic tastes, and of my sensual fancy. It is a villainously detached mind.

It goes on working in odious discontinuity quite apart from what I am feeling and saying.

It has also—this rational mind of mine—an infernal sense of humour. How it gets hold of this, God knows; for I had always supposed that humour was a thing connected with one's general idiosyncracies. My grotesque difficulties in dealing with "matter," the thousand absurd ways in which matter fools me and tumbles me about, are never missed—you may be sure of that!—by my goblin-like mind.

I would not reveal to others,—not for a kingdom—what this demon whispers to me, and the deadly shrewdness of its mockeries. I get no pleasure from its damned commentaries. You are quite wrong, dear reader, if you conjure up a charming little Sadistic complicity between this fellow with the whip, and my poor shrinking sense-consciousness. I implore him to stop his flicks and fillips; but he never will; he only goes on the more. I have to paralyze him by pretended indifference, or by rolling up into a sulky pachydermatous passivity, like a prickly hedge-pig.

My mind differs from the minds of my artistic friends in being so sceptically detached from my imagination. In this respect—and here I am sure I may speak without boasting—I am much more in-tellectually *honest* than these charming people. That they are so charming and that I enjoy them so, is due to this very cause. Thank Heaven they are not cursed with this diabolical Puritanism of the pure reason, which I find so devastating!

They wilfully and deliberately seem to keep plunging their minds into the exciting cisterns of their imaginative senses, and continually hauling them up, all phosphor-escent and glimmering—crusted over with the most lovely silt and shells. I wonder if they are as conscious as I am of the great pistons and driving-rods of Nature. Per-haps they are. Perhaps they are just as fatalistic and disillusioned. Only they say to themselves, "Since we all know the murderous uniformities of destiny, let us pretend a little, and colour our reason with the colours of our imagination!"

Now why is it that I so persistently re-fuse to do this, and continue to hold my reason so clear, so unstained by the sweet rich dyes of the sensual imagination?

I think the cause is not simple, but extremely complicated. It is partly a rigid point of morality with me,—not rational morality, but a sort of ingrained moral imperative, the breaking of which would tear my whole being to pieces.

It is partly my restless longing to escape from myself and from all human associations. The free unclouded working of the mind, in liberation from imaginative colouring, is itself a sort of escape. When I think in this dry, cold, detached manner, I become disembodied, impersonal, without love or hate, I become a mere "airy nothing" of analytical activity, suspended, as it might be, *in vacuo*, over the flowing stream of things; and, becoming this, it seems as though there were needed little more than a shock of psychic dissolution, to merge me completely in the unconscious elements.

Finally I think I discern in it a desire to avoid the teasing laborious effort, requiring so much buoyancy and energy, of the use of the reason as a controlling pilot or ship-master of the wave-tossed senses. I let my senses drift as they will, and my imagination drift with them like a forlorn passenger upon a derelict vessel; while my irresponsible reason floats away upon its raft, heedless and indifferent. On a former page I referred a little to my vices, and indicated that they belonged rather to the surface than to the depths of my being. In this view of the matter I am of course denying the great Schopenhauer's doctrine of the sinister profundity of the "Will to live." I am also denying the Nietzschean doctrine of the "Will to Power." In opposition to these formidable names, I may summon to my support those two calm and detached spirits, perhaps the wisest of all—I mean Epicurus and Spinoza.

But though my vices are on the surface, they are not the less imperious. It is on the surface that I "live and move and have my being." It is on the surface that I lead my queer subjective life of sense-impressions,—that life from which my errant reason is continually escaping.

So imperious indeed are one or two of these inveterate exigencies, that I sometimes wonder if the dullness of all this tiresome analysis is not due to the fact that I am not at liberty to blazon them arrogantly forth, in the manner of some unrepentant sinners in our midst.

Unfortunately the receptivity of our modern public is not as sane and shrewdly balanced as was that which welcomed the egotistic ramblings of Montaigne; and the result of this lack of balance in the public has not been encouraging in its effect upon more recent outspoken writers.

Those who do flourish their little vices abroad seem to be so disturbed by their consciousness of the public's attitude that their natural ease becomes brazen impertinence, and their honest self-analysis a ridiculous sort of swaggering bravado.

In their rage at their audience's grossness of apprehension, and in a savage wish to outrage it, they emphasize so monstrously the little perversities of their sensory nerves, that every kind of proportion is lost; and some quite harmless fool of a sedentary scribbler, whose real permanent instincts are most innocently domestic, steps forth upon the boards a terrible and awe-inspiring Don Juan. The stupidity of the public, with the contemptible baseness of its paid teachers, is really responsible for half the childish arrogance of our naive immoralists;

while a deplorable lack of humourous commonsense, on both sides, throws the matter out of all relation to reason.

A time will perhaps come again—may it come soon!—when the old, wise, classical way of regarding all these things, will lift such blurring mists and disfiguring mirages from the self-knowledge of men and women. But meanwhile, I for one, have not the remotest intention of turning my little peculiarities into great Satanic masks of anti-social defiance.

The very suppression of free speech in these things, which is so contemptible an aspect of our age, tends to excite in the average mind a most monstrous and vindictive curiosity; a curiosity untouched by any genial Rabelaisian humour; an evil, sneaking, hypocritical curiosity; a curiosity which is a bastard cousin to the worst excesses it reprobates.

The most sensible thing a writer or artist can do, is to "sublimate" what he regards as vicious in himself, and use it as a medium of illumination in his creative work. This alone, quite apart from social morality, offers a very plausible excuse for what is called "virtue," an excuse which the most inspiring among modern geniuses have not been slow to seize. Whatever may be said about the undesirability of vice in ordinary life, a certain amount of this smouldering Tartarean fire is absolutely essential in Literature. The absence or presence of it is precisely what makes the difference between an imaginative work and a work with no imagination, though in this also there are infinite and subtle degrees.

There is a certain vulgar sensuality in some popular writers which is odious. One flame of the Pit differeth from another flame of the Pit as widely as star from star. I say "flame of the Pit;" but there is really no need to drag in these portentous words. One writer has the genius to refine and winnow his aboriginal promptings to a noble imaginative issue. Another tosses them away in his track like bits of orange-peel from a proletarian picnic. Ultimately it is a matter of the difference between a fine taste and a taste of blundering indiscrimination.

I think I do plead guilty to certain quaint half-vices; things in no degree "wicked," but things which by their lack of intelligent suggestiveness must be regarded as belonging to the sphere of death rather than of life. Such for instance may be the queer semi-comatose sensuality which leads me to pace up and down, hour by hour, on the same grassy path or below the same sunlit wall. As I trail my feet along, the feeling of the earth or sand under them seems to have the odd diffused effect of some narcotic or drug. In the same way the peculiar and special look of a grassy bank against the sky thrills me, as I keep walking and walking beneath its shadow, with a weird, heavy vegetable sensuality. I seem to embrace its soft-flowing contours with a slow, Saurian persistence; not visualizing it in the least, artistically or imaginatively, but doggedly tightening my hold upon it, in a grave, quiet, patient obstinacy. I have a suspicion that there was something of this sluggish sensuality about the Wordsworthian attitude to Nature; only he used it for spiritual intimations, while I use it for its own sake and keep it a purely animal, or if you like, vegetable sensation.

Is it I wonder, because of this very heaviness and sluggishness of sensual apprehension that I cry out so wearily sometimes for the "wings of the dove?" What

I really do, I suppose, is to use earth and sand and dust, and grass and trees and flowers, as if they were things to be eaten and drunken, or things to be made love to, in a sort of mesmerized trance. I wish I knew by what gradual degrees, and exactly why, I have fallen into this habit.

I can remember long ago, on Dartmoor, astonishing and scandalizing my energetic friend T. H. L. by expressing a wish that there was no need for me to do anything ever again but walk up and down, up and down, a disused, moss-covered granite quarry.

My intelligent artistic emotions must be singularly abortive; and the delicate forms and colours of things must leave me lamentably unmoved; else I could never remain so long content, in a pure physiological ecstasy, absorbed by the mere material touch of the soil, and the mere material warmth of the sun. Was I really a great browsing ox in my last incarnation, or a broad-leaved placid burdock-plant?

I confess sometimes that the heavy, cynical, sceptical materialism of my temperament fills me with an immense repulsion. I am so accursedly self-centred and unhuman! It is not an agreeable sensation, dear reader, even for a master sensationalist like myself, to feel suddenly conscious of the absence in him of what everyone else possesses—the absence of a soul!

I catch myself envying sometimes the capacity for *natural sorrow* which normal people have. I verily believe that I could lose some of my dearest friends,—and still go on my way, kicking up the dust, and trailing my fingers through the tall hedge-parsley. I think I have something of the heavy, unilluminated obtuseness to feeling, of extremely old people. I believe I was born old. I certainly was treated as such by my childish companions.

It is out of the depths of this sluggish quagmire of dull sensationalism that I sometimes curse even the majestic fatality of the Universe. I think that if the feet of the god-like Nazarene ever trod the sandy paths of my frequenting, I should cast myself down before Him, and cry aloud to be delivered from "the body of this death."

Certainly, knowing what I know of myself, I will deal gently with every type of perverse and arbitrary egoism, with every mad mirage-hunter pursuing his own shadow across the desert.

I sometimes wish that I could be thrown into a kind of magical epilepsy, from the convulsions of which I should arise with a new soul and a responsive heart, and go forth to assume responsibilities, and to bear burdens, and fight fiercely for noble causes, and suffer the bitterness of love, and know the salt taste of tears.

How an attempt, such as this poor contradictory sketch, to indicate the perversities and frailties of one individual life, shows the barriers and inaccessible walls, between which we all grope forward, pushed so mercilessly from behind! It might almost seem as though the desperate, noble recklessness, with which our European youth is now throwing its life away, as a child's toy, at the command of its political leaders, is something more in harmony with the secret of Nature, than that avaricious hoarding up of imaginative sensations which is the life of the artist. Sometimes it almost seems as though only those who despised the preciousness of living, were those who really lived;—those only who held life lightly and risked it on the dice's throw; those only who really knew the true savour of its sweetness, and the spiritual thrill of its throbbing pulse. Certainly the path of our days leads to strange headlands now and then, looking over unexpected landscapes. Happy are those who do not see the image of themselves as a dark stooping shadow moving with greedy intentness across the pastures from fungus-bed to fungus-bed, and avoiding morosely the flocks and their shepherds. Happy are those who from such a promontory, over the valley of their pilgrimage, can see, not one dark image of themselves unchanged and unchanging, but a long procession of wayfarers, different and yet the same;—a procession of which their present living image is only one in an endless sequence, a sequence of the putting off of masks and the stripping away of disguises; a sequence of death for the sake of life, and of life for the sake of more life!

Happy are those; but, meanwhile, irrevocable Fate sweeps us all forward, and the wisest and least wise among us are lucky if they can adjust themselves to its adamantine decrees, without the aching of their flesh and the envenoming of their heart's

blood. It will be something, after all, if
when we die, though we have been the
maddest egoists on earth, some queer acquaintance be found to throw a handful of
dust upon our ashes, and to feel a moment's
darkening of the high sun in the indifferent
heaven, at the loss of even so unresponsive
a fellow-wayfarer.

CONFESSIONS
LLEWELLYN POWYS

FOREWORD

I DO NOT think these vague autobiographical ramblings should as a matter of fact
bear the title of Confessions. "Confessions" suggests that one has written about
one's sins—this I have not had the courage
to do. Instead I have endeavoured to
recapture from the past some of the simpler
sensations which have made up my life.

My thanks are due to the editors of
The New Statesman and *The New Age*
for allowing me to republish passages from
my diary which have already appeared in
their papers.

I

To be suddenly born, to suddenly acquire consciousness on the surface of this unsteady and amazing planet, that is a chance indeed to justify everything.

Life is a series of visions and sensations which by the wildest fortune it has been given us to experience.

Puritans are fond of the phrase "it is for us to do this or that" and it appears to me that it is for us merely to be irresponsible spectators of the drama of existence as it unrolls itself. Irresponsible however—that is the secret, that is the key to one's attitude in a world whose very foundations are so complex, so varied, so scandalously immoral. To an adventurous and imaginative spirit the world is as it should be, nothing confined, nothing explained, nothing impossible.

Of course if people endeavour to graft their own particular ideas of what life ought to be upon life as it is, they begin to sigh and grow grave immediately. Once however let a man come to understand "that nothing really matters," that there is no particular purpose in our corner of the universe, that the earth has but to circle the sun some seventy times and he is gone, and a new acquiescence will be born into his soul, an acquiescence which will give him time and taste to look around him and let the golden sand run through his fingers how wistfully!

Out here in Central Africa these truths are brought home to one continually. One has but to draw aside the tangled branches of these ancient overgrown forests to appreciate what kind of a world we live in.

In civilized countries the silly conceptions of silly people stifle our intelligence just as their drawing rooms stifle our lungs, but in this country where through terror the grass eaters never grow fat and where every night the striped fiery hunters feel the death throes of their prey one cannot be so easily deceived. Casualty, injustice, demoniac cruelty is patent: and to realize that these "goings on" have received divine sanction from the earliest ages it is only necessary to raise one's eyes to the sun as he rises in his splendour morning after morning.

I sometimes think that children if left to themselves understand the nature of the universe far better than grown up people. I think they look at the world in the right way, are more receptive and receive its experiences with more appropriate emotions. Those vague simple delicious memories of a child, so delicate, so evasive, are amongst the memories one would wish if there was a future life to carry away with one—the first glimpse of tiny blue eggs in a hedge sparrow's nest; the happy tints on summer curtains put up unexpectedly in the night nursery after the dreary winter rains; the soothing somnolent twittering of swallows when one was trying to go to sleep with all the sounds and scents of the garden coming in at the open window.

To a child also, the alternative—the terrible—is continually present. They are supersensitive to all those vague intimations of the unknown, of the supernatural, which even the most naturalistic of us feel sometimes—as when by ourselves we open the doors of empty darkened rooms. They understand the romance of the terrible, of the stark.

I remember when I was a child a black cat was hung on a Wellingtonia in a field opposite the nursery window. Village boys used to come and whip it. I cried and was miserable, yet the spectacle had for my imagination the suggestion of endless terrible things which might be going on in the great world outside where truth to say it is given to certain human beings to derive pleasure from whipping—and perhaps from whipping not only black cats.

Another terrible revelation came with the death of my sister. She was only a little older than myself. The week before we had been looking for linnets' eggs in the battle-field, pushing our way through the gorse bushes which were so prickly, and so yellow, and smelt so sweet in the April sunshine. I was taken into the spare room and saw her lying in bed, feverish and sick—she asked me how we were getting on with the house we were building in the garden and whether there were eggs yet in the chaffinch's nest at the end of the box hedge.

The next day as the rest of us were sitting under the shade of the Portugal laurel on the lawn, my brother, J.C.P., came to say that she had been taken away by the angels.

I know now that it was only the way he put it, that really he does not believe in angels and never did.

I think death alone—the mere report and rumour of it—brings home, in some degree, to the most inexperienced intelligence the fatal and exciting nature of our destiny, of the destiny of all living things who have each in their turn to go down into the pit.

At school under the shadow of the grey abbey I gradually awakened to the continuous poetry of life set as it was against so immemorial and romantic a background.

It was there too that I came to learn for the first time of the passionate and tremulous emotions which lie at the back and root of all life. Masters used to try to persuade one, in solemn conversations alone in the study, that these emotions were wrong, that their only *raison d'etre* was as a means by which God tricked the human race into prolonging its life generation after generation. Sexual excitement to this day remains for me a treacherous and scarlet background, but I now understand that all lapses in this direction should be treated with the utmost indulgence as being merely the expression of essential subterranean forces far more powerful than any of us. And as a matter of fact it very often happens that this strange and subtle ecstasy is alone capable of touching with a live coal the imagination of certain very stupid people.

For years I remained in the lower school dreaming over my school books, my mind as dim and unlighted as the monk-haunted classrooms where I sat; then suddenly I found myself "shoved" into the upper school, into the clear white light of Mr. R.'s classroom. The schoolmaster was not like the others—though curiously disillusioned as to the world in general, he was possessed by a passionate devotion for English Literature. I think he knew the Golden Treasury off by heart.

Over the chimney-piece where the boys collected before class was hung a photograph of the Apollo Belvedere, and those shapely white limbs have often seemed to be symbolic of the white light of that room as it shone upon and inspired my confused boy's mind.

In Four A, I read for the first time passages from Homer and Horace and came to understand from punctilious translations the strange magic latent in books. R.'s sarcasms made their impression. He used to accuse us of reading Greek History as if it was the history of black beetles.

He continually seemed to be hinting of a larger and more gracious world. I remember to this day the enthusiasm he displayed in quoting Matthew Arnold—I remember the very lines which he selected:

"Through the vex'd garden trees."
"The unplumbed salt estranging sea."

It was at this time that my brother, J. C. P., began giving me books. Much of the poetry I did not understand but again I got glimpses of a wider and freer and more magnanimous world than that presented to me by the official schoolmaster and by the school chapel. Certain passages of Swinburne filled me with a profane enthusiasm:

"But the Gods of your fashion
That take and that give
In their pity and passion
That scourge and forgive
They are worms that are bred in the bank
     that falls off;
They shall die and not live."

I began to take the spell of the school chapel very lightly—the spell of those queer intervals of silent prayer and of the dim lighted altar. I began to feel instead a thrill at the sight of the first celandine (for no other reason than that old Wordsworth had delighted in it) or at the sight of the hay fields by the river—yes, red with sorel as we wandered through them, our top hats in hands, some hot Sunday afternoon in June. In the holidays I used to stay with my brother Theodore, that strange and lonely being, who has never been under any illusion about reality and its worth and has come to learn so much melancholy wisdom in lonely places.

He was then living in a little village by the sea. In his house I could read what I liked and from him I imbibed a healthy distaste for the work of the practical every-day world and an inveterate love of quaint and profound thinking. Since then he has retired to a still more secluded village and I have never revisited Studland, but in my mind to this day a strange radiance and gladness seems to hang over the place—the radiance of youth and shimmering seas, the radiance of white chalk cliffs and wet moorlands, the radiance of children's faces and children's white frocks and the sad gladness of white sea birds crying to their young in clear sea sunshine.

And then I went up to Cambridge. Perhaps no experience should be more bracing to a boy's intelligence than his first entrance into a University.

To find one's self free to think and say what one likes is a privilege seldom permitted, but here in these antique rooms where there are no old people, the crass system of things is no longer so shielded. One comes across strange types. J., who kept human bones in his room and who would sleep all day and go down to the Union at night with a great pipe in his mouth and an outrageous shock of red hair over his grotesque "cerebralist" skull. L.U.W. (still after everything dearest and noblest of my friends), with his ardent antinomian philosophy and graceful Aubrey Beardsley appearance. D. of Corpus, whose ears and nails were always filthy and who used to spend weeks at a time drinking in low out-of-the-way taverns because as he said he liked to listen to the talk he heard in such places and liked to feel himself relapsing into alcoholic oblivion with these quaint human beings as a background to his dreams.

I remember perfectly well my first night in one of those old oak-panelled rooms—the weird sensation I got when raising my head I read on one of the beams supporting the roof the words "Pray for the Soul of John Cowper Powys." I had not known it had been my brother's room and this simple fraternal petition shocked me into understanding the grave and striking import of our lives as conceived by the one true Catholic Church. I knew that there were many people who held that my brother had no Soul. Now that I look back on those short three years I feel that I wasted my time. The actual world as I saw it seemed to absorb so much of my attention. We formed a club called the Club of the Honest Cods, and we used to meet on Sunday evenings in the old court and drink hot punch and sing bawdy songs.

Only at rare intervals did the old beautiful, cruel, gay, miraculous world reveal itself. I remember standing one afternoon by the side of the river not far from Mr. Benson's house envisaging the deep volume of still waters flowing on and on year after year so, so detached, so profoundly indifferent to the lot of the wisest of all the animals who had chosen to congregate on its grass-grown banks. And sometimes at the high noon of night looking out at the illumined mullioned College windows, the smooth grass and the shining ivy leaves, I would experience vague intimations of the murmuring Universe far, far removed from Corpus and from my rowdy every-day existence.

When I came down I spent some months at home receiving those queer little blue typed notices of academic vacancies from the scholastic agents, Gabbitas and Thing. I used to take these into my father's study and he used to look them over very gravely and sometimes before prayers as the family were sitting waiting for the servants to come in he would ask me if I had heard from Gabbitas that morning. At last a letter did arrive from the headmaster of a fashionable preparatory school on the Kentish coast, asking me to come down and interview him. I did so.

As soon as I arrived I was taken in to lunch in the school dining room. I remember it all very well. When table No. 3 was "put into silence" I felt exactly the heart-sinking of a new boy at coming into contact with the arbitrariness of a discipline which sends a shiver down the spine of many grown up people even. At other tables I saw "undermasters" carrying on conversations with the boys who sat next to them with that particular forced jocularity and super-ciliousness which is so noticeable to a non-academic mind—again my heart sank. The headmaster was a tall imposing figure. In the middle of lunch I took from my pocket a scrap of Roman pottery which I had found the day before in a mole hill on Ham Hill. It interested him and I think it was this that made him select me. I was to take the place of one of his masters for the summer term.

On the whole I recall those three months with pleasure. At first I was terrified at having to teach at all: all the little boys were cleverer than me. I used to have to steal along to the class rooms every night to get hold of a book "with answers" so that I might work out the sums we would do the next day, in the seclusion of my bedroom. I also had to do this kind of preparation with the Latin Prose and French—French! that was always terrible to me; most of the boys had been abroad and knew how to speak it quite well. The worst of it was a certain good-natured "Madam" who used to come over from Ramsgate twice a week to give conversation lessons, seeing my predicament got it into her head that it would be a kindness to let me attend her classes. A chair was placed for me at the end of the room and there I used to sit—like a great clownish dunce—while these clever children chattered to each other and to the lady. The mere possibility of being called upon to pronounce the simplest word made me literally sweat.

It sounds as I tell it as if the situation was after all not so very awful—but it was enough to make me miserable, it was enough to make me howl when I was by myself, it was enough to make me take a French grammar, concealed in my pocket, during those thrice precious hours when I was free to go where I liked.

I used to go off to Margate or Ramsgate by tram. In those places I could feel the ebb and flow of the great world—nothing here was closed down, nothing here was confined.

I might no doubt have had no end of exciting assignations at these times but I never did; it seemed quite enough for me simply to be there witnessing the manners, the comings and goings on the hot sands. Sometimes it is true as I paced along by the water's edge I did get glimpses which sent vague thrills through me— thrills exquisite and enervating. There is always something Pagan about the seashore: it is free and beautiful. Lust is there but it is the Lust of the open air and hot sunshine. At the end of the afternoon I would look out for some out-of-the-way teashop where I was sure not to be recognized and where I could eat watercress and shrimps at my leisure.

I would return again by tram car and as I went swaying along with that curious iron bar which I suppose connects the electricity, crackling and hissing, rising and falling, I would never miss a certain orchard which I could just see over a high wall—an orchard with midsummer grass and moon daisies and cowsparsley rising high under the apple trees and seeming to me to be typical of the kind of place of romance one is always longing to find oneself wandering about in, under quite new conditions, in another life almost.

And I had need to restore myself with places of romance, for besides the boys I had the undermasters to contend with. I don't suppose any young man who is worth anything would be content to spend his life as an undermaster in a Private Preparatory School, and no doubt this is the reason why one comes across such objectionable and imbecile types in such a position. There were four here besides myself. They were all golfers. T., a straight-forward and not altogether unpleasant type who had allowed his intellect to dwindle and dwindle from lack of use till he was capable of wondering how the "Futler," as they used to call the headmaster, could possibly give to the top form such free interpretations of the Old Testament stories. W., an international football player, very proud of his muscles and with the manners of a prizefighter—he used to get little boys to put their hands on his arm and then catch them as in a vice with his biceps. H., an insufferably conceited gentleman with a talent for rhyming after the manner of Gilbert and Sullivan.

The music master—I think now I could have made something of him—lank and lean, with crisp black hair cut short like a school boy's and with quite an exceptionally long nose; he was certainly more intelligent than the others and certainly more incompetent. But I hated them all, they were petty and mean and wearisome. I used to die at having anything to do with such people.

Every night coming from supper we had to walk down a long passage (I being junior to the others walked behind) at the end of which was hung that picture of the Laughing Cavalier which has in it such an extraordinary amount of Falstaffian, Rabelaisian earthiness. I used to look up at him and catch his eye—that eye that babbles of taverns and green fields, that libidinous and wine-bibbing eye with its generous assurance that after all undermasters did not make up the whole of life.

But they were devils! these undermasters, they did not appear to have any brains at all.

On one occasion I made my form learn that charming child's grace of Herrick's—I wrote it on the blackboard:

> "Here a little child I stand
> Holding up my either hand,
> Cold as paddocks though they be
> Here I hold them up to Thee,
> For a benison to fall
> On our meat and on us all."

By some ill-luck one of my colleagues (what a word! as J.C.P. remarked when I used it in one of my letters to him) came in and read it. You can imagine what shouts of laughter the recital of those lines created as an example of what "Po face" taught his form. "Cold as paddocks! cold as *paddocks*!"

They completed the school chapel while I was there. I would sometimes attend the early services and noted not without ironic interest how eagerly these schoolmasters would return after their devotional exercises to their toast and marmalade and hot coffee. How snug and well appointed that chapel was! A peer of the realm—whose pedigree is not unknown to me—presented it with an altar cloth costing seventy pounds.

After the sands and the white cliffs I think I look back upon the gardens with greater pleasure than anything else—they seemed so opulent of gorgeous midsummer flowers, like peonies and poppies and carnations. I used to love to escape to the garden, chuckling to myself, my head full of my own thoughts. I think wherever grass grows, wherever there is vegetation—trees and bushes and flowers—one can be happy.

My predecessor was returning the next term so I did not go back to that school again. I was again at home and again because no other profession presented itself. I sent out applications for scholastic vacancies. One day in November I received a telegram asking me to go to a school in Worcestershire. I sent a reply saying I would come the next day and then went off for a walk through Stoke Wood and over Ham Hill wondering what this new venture was going to be like. A cold late afternoon mist enshrouded everything and the path through the wood was slippery with mud and sodden leaves.

I arrived at my destination the next day just as it was getting dark. I was told to go to a house called "The Gates" where some of the masters lodged. They were all in school but in the senior master's room I found the remains of the tea they had just finished.

You know the uncanny feeling of entering a room from which people—strangers—have only lately gone: one is conscious sometimes of almost a physical impact as though the auras of the late occupants were still hovering in the air. The servant lighted a gas jet which flamed and sputtered and I sat down at the table in excited dejection and nibbled at a piece of plum cake. I looked at the bookshelves and my eyes encountered rows upon rows of soiled school books only too familiar. Lower down I did notice a few books of interest but these were all in such new "birthday gift" covers that they in no way reassured me. I noticed the works of Anthony Trollope in the World's Classics edition.

By the fire was an armchair and when I looked at it I could almost see the schoolmaster sitting there night after night having his last pipe before going to bed. There were two or three pipes lying idle on the chimney-piece.

And then my work began. This time I had to take a much larger class and the boys were by no means all gentlemen. A more slack and more slovenly lot I could hardly imagine. I was always telling them to clear up the classroom but it always seemed to me smothered in used up foolscap rolled into round balls; the desks were battered and carved upon and the fingers of all the boys were inky and their collars grimy and crumpled. I am afraid I taught them very little, every time I unlocked the classroom door I felt as if I was going into prison and something worse than prison. Once in a rage I determined to cane a boy. When I had made all arrangements and saw his bent body covered with curiously shiny trousers I could hardly raise my hand. At that time pain suffered by any sentient being seemed awful to me.

It is different now. This very morning standing in the heat of the day I witnessed unperturbed the merciless flogging of an ox because it was refusing to work and out of very despair had lain down.

I did cane that boy. His name was Pringle and he had red hair.

On the whole the masters here were a more dignified lot of men than at the other more exclusive school. The headmaster was I think exceptionally distinguished, I used to sit next to him at lunch time and he would always talk to me in a friendly intelligent way. The masters' lodging at "The Gates" I had most to do with and they were by no means the pick of the school staff. We used to have breakfast and tea and supper together.

The senior master, whose room I first was shown into, was very spruce and well groomed and spoke with almost a lisp. He evidently took himself and his work very seriously and considered himself a very responsible person. I came to hate him. He was capable of saying the most tedious things. Every day before going in to luncheon at the big school we used to collect in a little room hung with old school groups. We used to look at these: they were as the little man used to say "of perennial interest." Once he complained of gout. "I suppose," he said with a smug self-satisfied smile, "we have to suffer for all the port our ancestors drank" In reality he was an awful little cad who had never had any ancestors at all. He told us how he was a staunch supporter of the Conservative party in his suburban house near London and he kept deploring the action of the Government in giving a free government to the Boers after all the money spent.

I must tell you that going and coming from the school to "The Gates" we had to pass through a very poor quarter of the town, where one was compelled to look upon the most appalling sights of penury and gloom. I continually saw children so starved that they looked like apes, and once an old woman walked in front of me with her white hair half eaten away by lice—yet it was down these streets that this spruce complacent scholar of Emmanuel College used to trip (all pious pompous sneaks come from Emmanuel) quite oblivious to it all, with his roll of carefully corrected papers under his arm and his dapper well-fitting mortar-board on his head. It was in those days I began to read *The Clarion*, that paper of Robert Blatchford's which is at once so refreshing and so insipid.

Then there was another master from Downing—a much more interesting individual with a really diabolical physiognomy who had drifted into schoolmastering God only knows how. I understood from the first that he really did not care for any of these things, only for his dog—a Great Dane, which was a terror to me and to the town in general.

But even in these surroundings I again got moments of peculiar exultation. In the Easter term the spring began to show signs of its approach. I used to go for walks by myself sometimes on the Kidderminster road, sometimes on the Birmingham road. I remember being very elated once as I was returning westward by the appearance of that faint green faraway light in the sky, which Coleridge and Walter Pater used to love and which always seems so extraordinarily suggestive of Space and Eternity. I remember too my pleasure at finding red dead nettle and colt's foot, and also at the smell of the cut grass on one of those rare hot days in March when they were preparing the field for the School Sports. But these masters—one could never get far enough away from them or their point of view. On one occasion I asked C. to come out with me for a walk after supper. He consented with amused condescension. As we walked down the lighted street my eye caught sight of those soft shadows on the moon's surface outlined with peculiar distinctness. I remarked how strange it was to think of those cold dead mountain chasms being actually visible to us—so aloof as they were from our particular life, from the wet shining pavements along which we were walking, from the mud and the lamplight and the newspaper posters. It was cold and the little man was wearing a pair of woolen gloves. He rubbed his wool covered hands together and remarked that it was too cold for him "to feel sentimental over the moon!"

Eventually this second term did come to an end and I was free again. I now wrote to my father that I was tired of schoolmastering and wanted to earn my living by "writing for the papers"—a suggestion vague enough to frighten anybody. My father very generously acquiesced. However with his letter came another one offering me the post of Private Tutor to a boy of fourteen at H.

I was to be paid a good salary and the idea seemed to offer certain possibilities—

anyway it would be a new scene and a new sensation. I will quote from my diary.

II

THE DIARY OF A PRIVATE TUTOR

Wednesday, May 6th.

ARRIVED here yesterday. The discreet, ironic civility of the coachman who was waiting for me on the platform made me at once aware of my new social position—of the social position of a Private Tutor. The house is late Georgian and is overgrown with roses, jasmine and ivy; it has a slate roof and large sash windows. As I waited at the front door I noticed a wire-haired terrier standing under a tall fir tree; I neglected to raise my eyes to the branches above, where I might have detected the amused visage of my future pupil. He is large for his age. His steel-grey eyes appear to change colour just like a ferret's do when you hold it up. His narrow lips clearly reveal his spoilt ineffectual soul. I am not to sleep in the house; they have found rather nice lodgings

206

for me on the outskirts of the town a mile
away. Dinner in the evening was a repeti-
tion of tea, the same discreet overtures, the
same critical and intense scrutiny.

Thursday, May 7th.

Woke early, had breakfast at eight o'clock
and then walked by the side of an old disused canal which meanders through grass
fields. Arranged a programme of work
and was unutterably depressed at the sight
of each dreary and well-known school book.
Swore to myself that I would never enter
the hated profession again. After supper
took a long walk in the dark. Came to a
village churchyard quite white with cowsparsley, the delicate flowers casting a misty
gossamer veil over innumerable mounds.
As I sat there for a few minutes smoking a
cigarette I could not help wondering if the
dead, buried people all round had any kind
of existence. It was a moonless night, but
the sky was illumined by mighty suns reduced to mere specks of light in the infinite distance. I never can understand
how people find consolation in looking at
the stars. To me they appear profoundly
melancholy.

Monday the 11th.

A gloomy day; there has been thunder about. I found Herb Paris in some private woods belonging to people called Hussey. Their house, an Elizabethan building, was not far off, and as we crossed a field, heavy with drenched May grass, we saw a figure in black walking on one of the terraces. They tell me she was Mrs. Hussey, who had lost her only child—a boy of nine years—in the early spring. It rained all the evening.

Tuesday the 12th.

Went for a motor drive and had a picnic on the downs. Coming back there was not room for me in the car so I walked. You can guess how delightful that hour and a half was; trailing along through the white summer dust, with ground ivy crushed in my hands and the sights and sounds of the countryside all about me.

Wednesday the 13th.

Played tennis, but was all the time worried by the recollection of a letter I had posted in the morning to the secretary of the American University Extension Society.

They have asked me to go out for the Easter term and give a course of lectures on English literature and in my letter accepting their invitation I somehow managed to spell "needless" with an "a". This absurd mistake kept "taunting my mind," as village people say, and I was continually making faces to myself and mentally howling.

Thursday the 14th.

There is a bank clerk lodging also at Richmond Villa. This evening I talked quite a long time with him; like a double-dyed fool referring to the ignominy of my present position, which of course he did not understand.

Friday the 15th.

This morning we made a diminutive pond in the orchard. We then caught a number of unfortunate leather backed toads and made them swim in it.

Saturday the 16th.

Fell off my bicycle and bruised my knee badly. Rex absolutely refuses to walk and will not bicycle outside the garden.

He likes to steer his way round the narrow kitchen-garden paths with me behind him. I was doing this when I fell off.

Monday the 18th.

Tried to stir Rex's imagination by reading *The Burial March of Dundee*. Heard from my brother; he says: "To worry about 'neadless' is *needless* worry, for the Secretary will only think it a slip or a late English fashion!"

Tuesday the 19th.

We do our work in an upstairs room. We sit by an open window. From my chair I look across the lawn at three magnificent elm trees: morning after morning the intervening atmosphere is quivering with life— a myriad of gnats dancing in the hot sunlight. I wonder if they in their tiny life have invented Gods for themselves or if ever a single, great-hearted gnat has died for the rest.

Friday the 22nd.

Saw the tombs of the Earls of ———— A huge mausoleum standing on the edge of a hill overshadowed by cedars and over-looking a luxuriant Hampshire champagne.

The building itself was strangely chilling to the spirits, as such places usually are; one thought of the succeeding generations so free and powerful succumbing each in his turn, and being carried to this house of crumbling coffins and dead men's bones.

The absolute inevitableness of Death: one must never forget that!

Sunday the 24th.

Went to church and sat right at the back, next to the font. Periodically got a glimpse of my pupil and grinned like a lemur. In the afternoon played the fool with Rex and then walked round Bagnell with his sisters, discussing Socialism.

Tuesday the 26th.

As we were changing for tennis Rex threw half a glass of water at a little village girl who was passing below his window and had accidentally trodden on the edge of the lawn. I could have killed him as he stood there with his fat, flabby, half-naked body con-cealed behind the curtain!

Saturday the 30th.

Played tennis with two vulgar piano manufacturers, their hair plastered down with brilliantine, as I noticed when they bent down to alter the height of the net. I hated them. In the evening bought *The Clarion.* How refreshing after intercourse with these people to read the direct and downright writing of old Blatchford and Neil Lyons!

Sunday the 31st.

Cecily is dead in Paris. I was haunted by this all day long. She was seventeen and yet it seems such a little time since I used to see her at parties—a child immaculate, in dainty frock, blue sash and evening shoes.

Another horrible Sunday. "Pain is the choice of the magnanimous." "Pleasure is not an end in itself but rather an accident."

Wednesday, June 3rd.

Walked by the river and watched azure blue dragon flies glide here and there. Saw the reflection of an old mill in the water and from the mere joy of consciousness felt splendidly indifferent as to the future.

Saturday the 6th.

Rex insisted on catching dragon-flies and letting them loose in a hot-house. Was kept for supper.

Saturday the 13th.

Drove to a river three miles away. Rex fished, but could catch nothing. I walked behind, peering into the deep clear water, so different from that of our Somersetshire Parret. The meadows on each side were golden with buttercups. I longed for escape, I longed to wander forever through such fields!

Monday the 15th.

We are digging a deep hole in the spinney—a kind of smuggler's cave. It is extraordinary what satisfaction I derive from this occupation. There is something in the actual physical labour which makes me forget my abasement.

Tuesday the 16th.

A silly old major has come to stay in the house. He went through the Indian Mutiny and now in his dotage plays at being gallant with Mrs. T.

Wednesday the 17th.

Went to the Agricultural Show with Rex. He wore a white mackintosh and I was astonished to see how he had already acquired the insolent demeanour of the vulgar rich. It rained most of the time, but the flowers arranged inside the tents possessed amazing colour. I came across a farmer from our part of the country and longed to tell him to tell my brother that *he had seen me in Hell!*

Thursday the 18th.

Dug the hole.

Sunday the 21st.

Sat at the back of the church next a cripple with a pink bow in her hat. All these people must be absolutely mad; how could they otherwise be so dull and stupid in a world like this? In the evening read in the little front garden of the Villa. I helped my landlady water her flowers, geraniums, Canterbury bells and snap-dragons. The smell of the dampened earth very delicious. All the time village people were loitering along the road.

Thursday the 25th.

I have constructed a kind of tent in the little front garden. It is made by hanging blankets over an old clothes' horse. I have bought a lamp and read late every night, often marking the time and date on the margin of the book so that when I read the passage again I shall be reminded of my time of consciousness in this tiny garden.

Saturday the 27th.

A little cousin of Rex's arrived to-day. We three played together and I was perfectly happy in her radiant and animated presence. She is only fourteen years old. We showed her all the secret places in the garden—our hole, and the nests in the trees. She got very hot and asked me to carry her summer hat because the elastic was tight and hurt her chin.

Sunday the 28th.

Sat at the back of the church and then played in the garden. I was asked to conduct Mary to a friend's house. Our way was across fields and we walked side by side. It was very hot. In the tangled hedgerows no birds sang, only the shrill bat-like cry of field-mice was audible. She refused to go in at the gate but clambered over a high wall at the bottom of the garden, waved good-bye and vanished forever.

Tuesday the 30th.

Picnic supper on the Downs. Rex fell down and began to cry and I felt extraordinarily exasperated. Rather an attractive Scotch girl called Doris is staying here. She was at school with one of Rex's sisters.

Saturday, July 4th.

There was a party to-day—a fantastic affair—reminding me of the mad garden party in *Alice of Wonderland*. They all had more money than manners. I could not have conceived it possible that so many silly vulgarians could have collected together! One person alone attracted me; he was the parson of the place. We went apart and talked, and he with tears in his eyes spoke of Jesus—his Master. I could fancy him to have only just left Our Lord's side. He might have been walking yesterday with the twelve in Galilean lanes. I was amazed. "Here," I thought, "at last, have I come across somebody whose life is a reality—who is really alive!" I loved him.

Tuesday the 7th.

Late in the evening I escaped and ran off to the Vicarage. The priest was alone, his wife away. It was a beautiful night and we wandered about his garden, over his lawn and up and down his box-fringed path in the kitchen garden. We talked of literature and religion. Although his head is grey there is passion in his soul. The summer garden as we walked about in it seemed enchanted with its dim aromatic shadows and listening flowers—so enchanted that one could hardly believe that the dull importunacy of the routine of things would ever again obscure one's imaginative insight.

Wednesday the 8th.

It rained all day. We played hide-and-seek in the house. On one occasion I came upon Doris curled up in a linen cupboard, flushed and laughing and very provocative.

Thursday the 9th.

Played tennis in the rain at the doctor's house. Then ran off to my lodgings, hoping to get an evening to myself; however, they sent a motor, begging me to come to dinner.

Friday the 17th.

We all went to play tennis at the Husseys' —a very old family, tragic and doomed. The Squire, a man of sixty, has twice been in a lunatic asylum and has still the sullen, pre-occupied look of a homicidal maniac. He is a very big man with an immensely broad back, pale face and slobbering articulation. I walked to the end of the terrace with his wife—the lady in black—and she showed me her dead boy's garden, with the flowers he had planted and the border stones he had arranged.

Monday the 27th.

Only one more week and I shall be free!

Thursday the 30th.

We have motored down to Weymouth for the night. Just now I walked to the end of the pier; the lights from the crescent-shaped front shone like golden daggers in the sea. I am sitting in my bedroom near the open window: footsteps on the esplanade and the distant whistle of a railway train, shrill and weirdly romantic, are the only sounds audible above the surge and ripple of the sea.

Monday, August 3rd.

Free at last! Wished "Good-bye" to many people. In the evening was with my brother. We walked to a village five miles from his home and had supper there in a little back parlour. We had much to talk about. It was midnight before we got back, but we who are possessed never grow tired!

III

AMERICA

IT WAS now that I fell more completely than ever under the influence of my brother J. C. P. He had persuaded me to try lecturing in America and the preparations for these lectures brought us much together sometimes in Somerset, sometimes in Sussex.

I began to learn more and more about the world—to understand the miracle of corn-fields golden and bread-bearing and hot in the August sun; to understand the mystery of the sea, full of strange vegetation and shells and salt spray; and the old world melancholy of great woods and tidal rivers, and ancient country towns. We were together always. Every insignificant incident of the day was experienced with relish —the few minutes out in the garden before breakfast—the lighting of cigarettes as we hurried off together afterwards. The pouring out of tea at some Village Inn, with the road outside still light and dusty in the late afternoon.

We visited churches and peered curiously at the symbols and images that had meant so much to our race. We loitered and read the old weather-beaten inscriptions on the stones outside—we thought of Hardy and Shakespeare and of the still bones of the peasantry below in the earth. We stopped to watch village children dancing under the chequered shadows of old west country elms—to notice old labourers returning from the fields with stories of gladness and sorrow, of births and deaths written on their disfigured brows. And all the time the world unfolded itself before my eyes, this world of sun and rain, of sea and river, of churches and dead men's bones. We crossed the Atlantic together in the late Autumn and I looked out day after day at that huge track of heaving waters—there from the beginning and so large a part of the earth. I was amazed. This I thought is the world: vast lands and vaster waters and with what happenings going on here and there!

At the end of our journey we arrived at New York and I saw what the human race had done here. Like a giant city New York raised her illumined battlements in the darkness. I don't know that I actually learned much from America—it was staggering, astounding and seemed possessed of an exaggerated reality of its own. With such a spectacle before my eyes any just view of existence was blurred. I received the impression of a tireless, indominable people displaying absolute indifference to their fate—to anybody's fate; a people that rushed to and fro and entered upon the New Year, the New Year of each of their destinies, with hoots and rattles and catcallings. In a curious way they seemed separated from the rest of humanity: a race devoid of fear, devoid of reverence, whom it was impossible to associate with the tragic misused beings for whose sake it was necessary for a young Semitic God, noble and heroic, to die.

When I got back to England I had but a few months to spend before I became ill.

It seems to me now that I was particularly fortunate at that time. I was always wandering about in places where cuckoo flowers grew and where sea-poppies grew and where garlic was made white by the droppings of rooks. We spent two weeks I remember at Sidmouth in Devonshire under the shadow of those weird blood red cliffs, with sea gulls and overgrown inland hedges and rabbits pirouetting, fantastically silhouetted against the Atlantic—against Eternity. All the time a myriad microbes alive and active were eating away at my body, at my very life. Suddenly I began spitting blood, "There is no time to be lost," said the doctor, and I was hurried away to Switzerland.

My brother J. C. P. came with me. Together we listened to the sea on Dover beach; together we listened to the sighing of the wind in the house-tops of Laon before even the Germans were there. I quote again from my diary:

IV

A CONSUMPTIVE'S DIARY

November 29th, 1909.

I MUST be ill; last night I coughed up blood. I slept badly also, the sound of the wind and drifting rain keeping me awake.

What an autumn it has been! We have not seen the sun for weeks. All low-lying fields are flooded, all roads heavy with mud, and all trees black with dampness.

I am going to the doctor this morning. Probably I have broken some small blood-vessel and shall be all right in a day or two. I cannot help remembering, however, those ominous words of John Keats when he spat blood for the first time "I know the colour of that blood; that blood is arterial blood; it is my death warrant; I must die!"

Later. I have interviewed the doctor, and he says I have consumption and must leave England at once.

I asked if I might not wait till after Christmas, but he told me there was no time to be lost.

December 2nd.

I am starting for Switzerland next week. My eldest brother is going to travel with me. I have still discoloration and slight fever.

December 9th.

We got here yesterday, having broken the journey at Basle. I have never been abroad before, so that, in spite of my weakness, I found the journey extraordinarily exciting.

Amazing! suddenly to see in reality the historic continent of Europe, for me hitherto only a matter of maps and writing. At first I looked out upon the plainlands of Normandy—that country so dear to Guy de Maupassant—with its limitless fields and small workaday farms, and afterwards at the more undulating landscape of the frontier, with now and then a swollen river sweeping along quite near to the railway line.

We had our first glimpse of the mountains coming up to Landquart, formidable grey granite cliffs overhanging slate-coloured lakes—scenery sombre enough and well selected for Pontius Pilate's legendary end.

At last, as it was getting dark, our train ran slowly into Davos Platz station. A crowd of porters, each with a name of a sanatorium or hotel inscribed on the front of his hat, stood waiting at the end of the platform.

Eventually we were conducted to a sleigh and driven up here. As we passed through Davos we could see on every side prostrate figures on lighted balconies. My room, No. 14, is a fairly large one. (The fact that No. 13 is completely omitted strikes me as an astonishing concession to the superstition of the modern European.) Exactly opposite, on the other side of the valley, rises a huge fir-clad mountain, with curious straight paths running down its precipitous sides, used, so I am told, by woodcutters for sliding timber. I am to stay in bed for at least two or three weeks, so as to become acclimatized to the rarified mountain air.

My brother leaves to-morrow.

December 10th.

This afternoon I was examined by the doctor. He says my chances of recovery are good.

As I looked down upon his bald head, busy with a stethoscope at my chest, it seemed extraordinary that one skeleton man by merely listening could possibly predict the longevity of another.

December 15th.

To-day I was allowed on my balcony for a few hours. From my *liege* chair I could see a small village at the bottom of the valley, a village in miniature, with flat-roofed houses clustering round a tiny church. In all directions the mountain sides are dotted with châlets.

December 20th.

This morning I went down to the dining-room for the first time.

I sat at the English table between two men who had got the thing in their throats and could only communicate in whispers. One of them, a sentimental clerk from Newcastle, tried to enlist my sympathy by writing on a scrap of paper "I am a married chap." There was an Anglican priest also at the table, a sly whimsical High Church-man, plump as a partridge, but with death obviously upon him.

December 21st.

I went down again to-day and am getting to know the various people by sight.

There is rather an attractive American woman at the table opposite; she is married, but seems just now very much occupied with a dour-faced Scotchman. At another table, a little farther away, sits a Hungarian—a graceful serpentine figure strange-ly emaciated. There is a young Russian also—a fellow of Herculean proportions, with heavy Slavonic jaw and expansive gestures; he is in love with a little compatriot of his, a beautiful barbarian, slender and delicate, with pale ivory hands and black lynx eyes.

I have named her the Hamadryad, and in truth her voice possesses something of the quaint shrillness of a wood-creature. For the rest the room is filled with a curious medley of degenerates from every country in Europe—philosophic Germans, flushed and friendly; smartly-dressed foreign-looking Frenchmen, and aristocratic Austrians.

December 22nd.

Walked up and down the terrace. The cold freshness of the air when one first comes out is very delicious, and I begin to feel better. I encountered the priest who made jocular allusions as to the gravity of his health, but even so, I saw the death terror at the back of his eyes.

December 26th.

Went down to the Christmas dinner last night and sat next the Hamadryad, who, I fancy, was drinking too much champagne. I amused some of the patients afterwards by telling fortunes. "Your life-line is a good one," I said to the Hungarian. "Good one, good one!" he laughed, "That's funny, considering I am dying!"

He is a strange type, subtle and irresponsible, and declares himself a disciple of Montaigne. Like so many other Europeans he has fallen under the spell of Napoleon; his room is packed with histories of that period and with busts and pictures of the great man. "There," says he pointing to the crowded relics, "there is the past; and there," indicating his table strewn with papers and musical instruments, "there is the present; and there," and now he pointed to his bed, "and there is the future!"

The death-mask of Napoleon, plastic and monumental, lay on an ebony stand by itself. He noticed that it had caught my attention. "I have often sat watching that for hours," he said. "That is rest."

January 1st, 1910.

The whole sanatorium is immensely diverted by the behaviour of the Russian. This great boy-giant has conceived a grand passion for the Hamadryad. He showers her with choice and costly flowers and this evening summoned the Davos band for her entertainment.

For all this she takes precious little notice of him—in fact she has told me she does not care about him. While waiting for the post this evening the priest began likening the sanatorium to the cave of Polythemus. "We are devoured one by one!" he said. Certainly his religion does not seem to reconcile him to the idea of death. I reminded him that Ulysses and a few of his men did at last escape clinging to the bellies of the sheep.

January 17th.

It has been a glorious day. The sun in the sky seemed smaller, but at the same time far brighter than it does in England, and under its rays the white frozen mountains gleamed and glittered. "True Davos weather," the habitués call it. I passed by many châlets coloured a rich mellow brown by the heat of the sun. The Russian is as infatuated as ever; it is really laughable to observe him at meal times trying to look at her without being detected by the other patients. She does not appear to notice him at all.

January 26th.

This morning out walking I amused myself by watching the peasants sliding tree-trunks down the mountain sides. They use a kind of single pick-axe, which they dig into the trees, shouting in gruff unison so as to strike and dig at the same moment. These were the weapons used against the Austrians.

January 28th.

The Hamadryad has been taken ill. I am sorry, as I have found her wild and wilful personality strangely fascinating. I was quite surprised to discover how startled I was this morning by coming across her name written in the snow; it was like finding the foot-print of a drowned child on the sea-shore.

January 31st.

The Hamadryad much worse. Report says she may not recover.

I went a walk in the morning, but have come to hate these mountains of sorrow.

From an open space in the woods I looked across a deserted white plain at Davos. There it stood, that city of dreadful death, forsaken, forlorn, and shrouded in shame. In the immediate foreground was the black spire of a church; and beyond, the enclosed piece of ground where so many unfortunate patients congregate for the last time.

Next week we are going to have a fancy dress entertainment. I shall procure a costume from Davos.

February 2nd.

My temperature by no means normal. This morning as I was putting on my snow-shoes I overheard a queer conversation.

The room next door has for some weeks been occupied by a young Englishman. Last night he had a bad hemorrhage. I guessed it was so, because when I woke I heard him give those successive gasping coughs which were absolutely unmistakable. Apparently the doctor was with him, for I heard him ask in a querulous tone whether he was going to die. For some moments the noise of the nurse emptying basins was the only sound audible. Then at last came the "No, certainly not, certainly not!" from the doctor.

He was dead by the evening though.

February 4th.

Walked along the path above the sanatorium. Kept digging my alpine-stock into the snow and admiring the blue colour like that of a breaking wave to be seen in the hole where it had been. A peasant passed leading by a rope an absurd mouse-coloured cow; he was bearded and smoked a long and hanging pipe. The fancy dress entertainment is to-morrow.

February 5th.

What a scene it was, this fancy dress ball!

I stood at the end of the lighted hall dressed as a Welsh prince in scarlet and gold, and there passed by countless fantastics, a nun, a bride, a pierrot, and an emperor.

Everybody in the highest spirits—cigarettes, champagne, laughter, and flushed cheeks. If it had not been for the continual sound of coughing, like the voice of a hollow-toned stranger, now here, now there, one would never have suspected that all was not well with this gay and coloured picture.

But this fact was brought home to me when, going up to my room for some forgotten object, I happened upon a group of servant men taking the opportunity, now that the corridors were deserted, to carry away a corpse. I only saw them for one moment; but I knew directly, as though by instinct, what they were at, with their oblong burden, their hushed voices, their stockinged feet. It is said that coffins of every size are stored in the sanatorium to facilitate the secret removal of bodies to the dead-house in Davos. For, after all, it is not pleasant to live patients to meet dead patients coming down stairs!

February 8th.

The Hamadryad is dead. It was her they were carrying away last night. The death of a guest is never announced in a sanatorium until the corpse has been removed. It is necessary to diminish the startled shock such news give to the others. When a day or two has elapsed, like silly sheep in a butcher's field, they can be re-assured.

February 14th.

Yesterday I drove down to the village in the valley. It was a wonderfully beautiful morning, but it turned off in the afternoon. I went inside the church; it was Zwinglian, and the interior was bare and desolate except for faded floral wreaths hung here and there in remembrance of the dead—a place more discouraging one could hardly imagine.

Coming back the sky was overcast—the mountains appeared chill and sombre and small flakes of snow began falling. I am quite glad to get back to my room again.

February 15th.

I think the extra exertion must have been too much for me, for to-day I am in bed with a rising temperature.

February 28th.

Yesterday evening the Russian shot himself, but by a strange irony, owing to his illness, his heart had moved from its right place, so he is not dead.

March 2nd.

I am getting worse.

March 10th.

Still no improvement. It looks as though my dissolution is to be a rapid one. The doctors sound me and give not unfavorable reports, but from their queer, calculating looks, I understand what they really think.

April.

This is terrible! I had no idea that I should come to fear death as I do. The whole perspective of my view of life has changed. It is as though I had been asleep or hypnotized all this time, and had only now waked, and what an awakening!

April 10th.

2.30 a. m. Hemorrhage! I see blood; I taste blood; I breathe blood! Will daylight *never* come?

V

VENICE

AFTER this hemorrhage I gradually began to get better. At last I was able to go out again, to look down at the little white buttressed church in the valley and see the peasants come and go from its gates like tiny ants. I knew they went there to worship God but I did not know whether they were wise or not. I made a scratch on the plastered wall of a châlet and used to look at it and wonder if I should ever see it again after I got back to England—this tiny scratch on this particular spot of the material universe. At last I was released and rushed back to England. It was May Day when my brother and I looked out of the hotel windows at Folkestone. How familiar, how delicious, how green everything looked, I could almost see the birds' nests in the hedges, could almost smell the young elder leaves as we were whirled up to London. My illness had sharpened my wits. At

night when I looked at the stars, I understood the background which belonged to
our planet, poised and sailing from mystery
to mystery, from Abyss to Abyss. I liked
the idea of the blank flaring spaces of infi-
nity giving birth unwittingly to crafty
intellectual eyes which peered out upon
their secret astral chambers. The planet
itself was sailing on to extinction either by
some catastrophic celestial collision or by
slow senseless withering, and each man,
each woman and each child was destined
also sooner or later to wear white stockings
and be carried away to the church yard.

When I sat in Church and heard my
father speak so certainly of a future life—
this was the future life I envisaged, while
the lamp light changed to a richer colour
the yellow Ham Hill stone of the Chancel
arch and the foolish village people grew
restless for their suppers and the boys and
girls lolled in their seats and sighed for
one another. I was a whole year at home,
then all of a sudden I found myself im-
merged in a great wave of apathy. I have
never quite been able to explain the cause
of this. Was it as my brother put it that
"the iron of consumption was at last

entering my soul" or that my enforced in-action was dulling my capacity for pleasure? Who can tell? who knows where these great clouds come from—these clouds which come sailing out of eternity and settle sometimes so heavily on the heads of the sons of men. When as I sit writing now, with the scoriac escarpments of Africa around me, I recall those days, it seems perfectly incredible that any sadness of the kind could have overtaken me, free as I was to wander over the station fields with brown hares circling through the gleaming windblown spring grass, with moor hens dabbling in the water and with the noblest of women by my side.

But so it was. When I went out in the early mornings, I no longer wanted to smell ground ivy, to smell the very earth itself, my imagination seemed suddenly drugged, my senses seemed to have lost their finer edge and the dead weight of the commonplace dragged me down and filled my spirit with lamentable misgivings. I wrote to my brother in a curiously peevish tone. I accused him of deserting me. I told him he had forgotten the roads, the lanes, the wayside trees, the field ponds we

had so often visited together. I told him
that I believed it was now of no conse-
quence to him that the purple lilacs were
already out by the side of the Fosse Way
and casting spiral shadows on the white
May dust. He came to see me at once and
suggested as we sat in the corner of the
potato garden, that I should go with him
to Venice. It was arranged. Before I
started I went down to the terrace walk and
picked for a buttonhole one of those spotted
Turkshead lilies, which possess such a deadly
and voluptuous and heavy perfume. It
was symbolic: it was what Oscar Wilde
would have done and that was why I did it.

We crossed the channel in Halcyon
weather. We reached Venice the next day.
Venice! I don't think any human apathy
could oppress me for long in that city—
day followed day and I walked those marble
piazzas in a kind of trance.

We climbed to the top of the Campanile
and looked down upon the apostolic croco-
dile and upon the lion. We went over the
glass factory and saw the workmen twist
the heated crystal into a thousand exquisite
shapes; we crossed to Torcello and wandered about the marshland behind; we

visited the Island cemetery and loitered down the long cypress alleys tapping at the marble walls each one honeycombed with the dead. At night we glided through the city in a gondola while ever and again out of the lapping water rose unmistakable the smells of old long forgotten centuries.

Sometimes we would wander into St. Mark's and on one occasion I remember we saw an old man shuffle up to the great pagan font and dip his fingers into the holy water and make the sign upon his forehead and upon the forehead of a child who was holding to him. We watched him there in the shadowy West End of the ancient church while all the time far up above the altar, the gilded angels sang hallelujahs to their creator, to the creator of Venice, to the creator of the world. The most trivial things seen during those days seem indelibly imprinted upon my mind.

I have forgotten nothing. I recall exactly the direct momentary glance of an elaborately dressed cosmopolitan harlot—so steely and ice-cold that it seemed to penetrate to my very soul as I prowled one evening up and down the brilliantly lighted colonnade. I remember also the look of a girl eating a handful of red currants in a shady and insanitary side street. I remember the June roses in the gardens on the Lido and the extraordinary knotted-skinned, spiral shaped sea horses—so miniature yet so perfect in design—which used to die by hundreds amongst the fishes dragged in from the Adriatic.

But all the time I was conscious of my sickness. It was always at the back of my mind. I could never dismiss it. I had a relapse on my way home and was laid up at Milan for weeks. For a whole year afterwards my health was uncertain. In desperation I decided to exile myself out here in this abandoned and sun seared continent. To be alive in Africa is better than to be dead in Europe. "We are still on the same planet," writes J. C. P. "but that is about all that can be said." I left England a month after war had been declared.

VI

FROM MONTACUTE TO GILGIL

September 4th.

TRAVELED up to London. Slept at Chiswick in a little back garden. The moon was in the sky and the pear trees were everywhere. Motored up to Blackwell docks.

Set sail at noon. We were held up outside Tilbury for some hours.

Across Essex flats I could see a church tower tranquil and with the afternoon sunshine upon it.

September 5th.

There are tiresome people at my end of the table. Opposite sits a lady who looks like a prostitute with her fixed beady eyes and immobile perfumed breasts. A little way off, however, there is an English parson —a typical public school man—whose appearance is as familiar and reassuring as an oak tree or Norman arch.

September 7th.

A horrible night! I could not sleep at all, was sick continually. The curious wishy-washy smell of the cabin nauseated me. I tried to drink soda water and was sick. I tried to eat grapes and was sick. Crept out on deck as soon as it was light and was confronted by an ice cold grey sea rolling and heaving as far as eye could see.

Lay in my deck chair all the morning watching white waves on the very borders of the horizon rise and fade and be submerged forever.

September 9th.

Watched the sun go down behind a wall of black clouds. Rays of light fell in lines upon the water where a single bird was flying—a mere dot in the sky.

September 11th.

Slept on deck. In the morning a sailor showed me a flying fish which had got stranded on deck. I liked to see its sharp spikey fins. All day there were shoals of them skimming over the waves, flying not for the joy in their hearts but for the terror.

September 12th.

During the afternoon we were all excited by the appearance of a huge ship on the horizon. It made as though it would round us up. However to our great relief it turned out to be British.

September 14th.

During the morning there were two torrential downpours of rain and we all had to seek shelter. In the afternoon a bird with black and white bars and crested head appeared suddenly flying after the ship. It was a Hoopoo. Other little birds alighted on the gunwhale, also moths fluttered about the deck. Evidently we were not far from land.

September 17th.

All night the sea was illumined by strange submarine lights shimmering now here now there, like a kind of water lightning.

September 18th.

Sat talking with the Eurasian doctor—a charming fellow with a bald head, bushy black moustache and a skin like old ivory. "When we are dead we are dead," he said,

laughing the hissing serpent laugh characteristic of Indians.

September 19th.

Sighted Ascension Island at eleven
o'clock. I lay on my couch at the back of
the ship and watched the mountains grow
larger and larger and turn from grey to
blue and from blue to mauve. The Island
is volcanic. It looks as though it had only
just cooled down from a molten state and
that the sea must still hiss round its rocks.

Above us sharp-winged swallow-tailed
seagulls sailed to and fro and below in an
indigo sea great finned sharks were cruising.

September 22nd.

In the morning approached St. Helena;
red scoriac cliffs rising bolt out of the sea.
Went on shore but could get no carriage to
take me up to Longwood.

Drifted up the main street, and very
desolate and dilapidated it was, with old
black trots, dusty chickens and lean cats
everywhere. As I was being rowed back
to the ship I noticed the dry cracked dirty
feet of the negro and thought how like they
were to the claws and hoofs of animals, with

their toughness and clinging discolored nails.

September 24th.

Woke early as silent moving figures were swilling down the deck; watched the white dawn spread over the sea.

In the afternoon sat talking with the Ts. What has made this fragile girl an atheist?

September 26th.

An albatross appeared—a single albatross —and kept sailing after the ship with beautiful owl-like curves, its wings wide outstretched.

I had my dinner by the light of the moon, as all the ship was darkened from fear of the Germans.

September 27th.

Talked with the little doctor who is going out to investigate the tsetse fly, and learnt from him how we are surrounded by innumerable minute intelligences. In the evening sat next Mrs. T. She did not want to go to bed when her husband arrived, so she caressed his hand. "See how I am bullied, Mr. Powys, forced to go to bed." "I am not forcing, I am only persuading." I remembered Nietzsche's words, "*All women are either cats or birds.*"

October 1st.

Capetown.   It rained in the morning, but by twelve o'clock it began to look brighter. I went into the town and walked up the green avenue and into the gardens. The gravel was steaming and there were heavy scents in the air. Came upon a statue of Cecil Rhodes looking very absurd with its black baggy breeches.

October 3rd.

Wasted all the day waiting to set sail. As a matter of fact we did not get off till six o'clock. I stood near Dr. H. as we sailed in the direction of the sinking sun, which was making all the lower part of the sky yellow; behind a full moon was rising, pale lily-white. Nietzsche hated the moon. He called it "sly cat of the roofs piously silently stalking over star carpets."

"We have strayed like lost sheep, we have followed the devices and desires of our own hearts." Why not? Why ever not? "Forgiveness!" "Salvation!" What do they mean? Why salvation? Why forgiveness?

Forgiveness for what? So we chatted on as we glided past the Twelve Apostles in the cool of the evening.

October 4th.

Sat talking with H. He remembered well seeing a yellow ray of the sinking sun shine through the muslin curtain of his nursing home and thinking to himself that there would be no more sunshine for him the next day.

"I was suffering pain," he said, "It makes me angry now to think how much pain I was suffering—useless, useless pain. What a creation it is! Think of it, consider it for a moment. God creates animals, but carniverous animals also. God creates fishes, but carniverous fishes also: the whole of creation is harassed in this way. That explains why in East Africa the animals have no fat on them—they are too harassed to grow fat even."

October 5th.

Very rough in the early morning. I talked with Dr. L., the entomologist—a little alert man who was surely an insect himself in his preincarnation.

He told me how the tropical jungle was teeming with life; how every twig and branch was alive, not only on the surface but inside also; how the evidence of the underworld as to the existence of God was ever ambiguous, was ever a yea and nay. He told of the driver ants and how they drive all before them, how even elephants turn out of their way and how on many different occasions he had observed a rapid migration of all creeping things before a column of them, mice and rats running for their lives and grasshoppers leaping and leaping.

October 6th.

Reached Durban at 6 o'clock. Observed the public buildings by their lack of originality reflecting exactly the Colonial taste. I wandered away down odd by-streets full of men with dusty birds' claws for feet.

October 10th.

At breakfast saw a turtle paddle past us with absolute aplomb, its brown shell gleaming in the sunshine.

In the evening sat talking with Miss N., and nodded with ennui, ennui.—Some women are intended for embraces alone.

October 14th.

In the morning a warship appeared on the horizon. She turned out to be British and soon after she had passed we changed our course to the south of the island. By two o'clock we were lying off Zanzibar, the remains of the unfortunate Pegasus still visible. I went on shore. The streets narrow and cool, almost like passages; the doorways decorated with Arab carving; within, cavernous shops with bright-eyed Indians squatting about in them. Curious the unmistakable smell of Arab towns— a sweet smell—a smell of silken oriental tapestries and brown and black humanity.

October 15th.

Woke as a strange rose-colored dawn spread itself over Zanzibar.—The pale crescent of the moon was under its spell, so were the motionless clouds, so also were the tropical shaped cocoa nut trees which fringed the farther hills.

October 16th.

Arrived at Mombasa and after some difficulty got my luggage through the customs and settled myself in the Uganda train. By the next morning we had left behind the dry scrub country and were crossing vast grass plains with the sun drenching down upon them. One saw many wild animals, hartbeests, giraffes, zebras and gazelles. From time to time the train stopped at stations and we looked out at Indians, at queer black men with decorated mangled ears, at tin-roofed houses and at burning hot earth.

October 18th.

Arrived at Gilgil, a place twenty miles from the equator with an altitude of 8000 feet. The sun went down and immediately the darkness echoed and quivered with weird unfamiliar sounds.

It is certainly an amazing country, this country of midnight murmurs, of burnished ebony men, of spotted golden-haired animals—a country vast, profound, inexplicable.

What beast, for instance, gave utterance to the agonized terror-stricken screams which I heard in the forest at the back of the house, and why are the cedar trees so gnarled and strangely bearded, and who

made that iron rock for the cold black mountain stream to flow over here in a country
where no church towers are and no pear
trees grow?

VII

AFRICA

October 19th.

WAS TOO excited to sleep much. I woke often and listened in terror to the sounds of the jungle. What is going on out there in the green darkness?

October 20th.

Rested all day on the verandah. W. brought me a lizard to look at, which he had caught in the garden. It had a green back and the eye of a demon. Its ancestors must have been revolving some queer thoughts for it to have acquired an expression so dragon-like and cynical. At night some boys came to say that "a dead kakapo was stinking like a dead porcupine." These natives will never approach a dead body: on their own reserve they get over the difficulty by dragging the dying to the hyenas.

255

We went out and set light to the whole hut. It burnt furiously. The cedar trees stood clearly outlined against the black sky. A white native bullock came and surveyed the scene with mild curiosity.

October 25th.

Heard a hyena howl for the first time in my life—a long low howl merging into a kind of whoop. I looked across at the outline of the black forest where the little tree irrisors were piping. Before I went to sleep Orion had risen away to the west.

October 26th.

Walked down to the rocks. What a country it is! It is always Africa! a strange terrifying country, a country inhabited by clawed creatures, by creatures with striped and gilded pelts, a country where even the moles are as large as water rats, and where the very nettles sting like wasps.

October 31st.

In the afternoon I sold my dove-coloured flannel suit to a negro who wanted to make love, not in Venice as I did when I bought it, but in Naivasha.

November 2nd.

In the afternoon walked with W. to the top of the escarpment. The long grass and clumps of trees almost suggest English parklands. Came upon some elephants' dung. We returned by a game path through cool moss-grown places of the forest. I tripped over a large bone gleaming ghastly white in the spangled sunlight. W. shot a wild duck. I picked it up. It wagged its tail, stiffened its webbed legs and opened and shut its round brown eyes, but I did not care.

November 5th.

Rode the mule to the swamps. A white flamingo rose out of the rushes and floated away with graceful tilted head.

When I came back I found the tabby cat lying on the verandah panting miserably and with its hind quarters crushed. The boys would not kill it. I got a saucer of milk, but it would not drink. "Kweda," said the cook, and it crawled with its front legs, mewing. I tried to write but could not. At last I compelled myself to kill it, flogging it with a heavy cedar stick. A few blows and it was dead with its mouth a little open and its limbs extended. I was reminded of another scene.—A human being's death or a tabby cat's death, it is the same.

November 8th.

Had tea at the B.'s. It was dark before we got back. Masharia came to meet us with a lantern. W. went to Abdulea's hut to see if he could buy any eggs. I sat on the mule outside observing Cygnus flying across the Milky Way.

November 10th.

Walked to the further shamba and then home. W. killed a bullock for the boys. He shot it with his rifle and it fell and rolled over with its legs in the air. The Swahilees cut it up. I peered into its reeking carcass and saw its pink lungs, its yellow dung filled belly and red gasping windpipe. The natives crowded round like black vultures, like hyenas.

November 20th.

B. arrived. He shot a monkey. He threw it down on the verandah where it lay, a little heaving man with black pads for hands and a long white tail.

We all three slept on the verandah. "You don't believe then in religion?" "Sirrah thou art said to have a stubborn soul, that apprehends no further than this world and squarest thy life according."

November 26th.

Received a letter from J.

"I can't get over your remoteness. We have on our mantel piece that Machiavellian picture of you with stick and hat. It looks at me as one who would say, 'Strike out and use your horn old fool.' O strange and hidden power of Destiny, how all is different now, all, all, all. These Germans are perpetually digging themselves in. Like great stinking badgers they run to earth at every chance. I've just been looking at some pictures of the Indian troops. What noble faces! I think I have never seen such noble human countenances anywhere. The Sikhs, I suppose. If the war does really mean that the East is moving at last and saying to the West 'Civilization thee ownself', I think it is a good thing. If men have noble, generous, brave and beautiful faces it must be right that they should conquer, eh? So much for the German sausages, for by God they aren't a lot of Goethes if these pictures represent them."

December 5th.

In the evening there was a dispute between two natives over a woman. All three came into the room. I heard the girl's voice and recognized at once the purring cat's voice of a woman. What matter though her buttocks be velvet black instead of velvet white?

At night W. went out after porcupines with lanterns and boys and dogs. I was asleep when he returned. He had dragged one back for me to look at—a great heavy badger-like brute stuck all over with quills. It had a rattle at the end of its tail and its head was large and heavy and Rhino-like.

December 12th.

R. and A. came to tea. I watched the three of them ride away, then strolled out towards the forest. I sat on a charred log. Natives shouted to each other, humped backed cattle browsed on the dry grass and the sun slowly went down over Africa. In the evening a letter from J. "Everyone is very quiet on the ship, as if the wind were blowing over its hosts of dead, crying and going (all of them) towards the race at Portland. The spring and élan seems out of everyone.—the Spring! Shall we ever see the lilacs again as we walk down to the village to post our letters, and back by the Park?"

December 20th.

I came back and set off at once for the forest where leopards had killed a buck the night before. I followed slowly behind. I found them setting the trap on the other side of the river; everywhere fragments of buck were strewn on the ground, the four legs, the ribs, the vertebrae.

December 29th.

I went shooting. I rode the mule over the escarpment up a narrow path. A herd of zebras were quite close to us.

January 6th.

Went shooting monkeys in the afternoon, but saw none. Sat on the ground in the forest. A few birds sang, but not like

English birds. In every direction strange white-trunked trees rose from the green brushwood. Set leopard trap. It was a dark windy night.

January 7th.

Went down to the leopard trap before breakfast. Coming over the hill we saw a spotted skin. It was a young she-leopard dead, shot through the eye. I smelt its warm yellow pelt and looked at its claws and teeth. Willie carried it home on his back. I walked behind stuffing stones into the hole in its skull to keep its brain from falling out.

January 9th.

T. sent me a letter he had from G. "Robin goes to school for the first time; but it's when a child gets 'alone' with the other boys that the Universe pinches him with its clumsy great finger and thumb. What a world! Christ! and God, what a world! How many playful little scenes of pinching and prodding are occurring on this side and that.—Lulu, damn his sly soul! loves to have it so and has gone off to put up silky leopards and rule over Somali tribes."

After dark I noticed a fire far away in the forest opposite. I asked the boys what it was. They said "Mungu" (God). I believed them. I could see him there well out of the way, warming his hands under the gaunt cedars. "Who is Mungu?" I asked. "Mungu lives up there," they answered, "and if he wants you to die you die, and if he wants you to live you live."

January 11th.

Caught an eagle in a gin. It was brought to me and laid on the verandah. Its legs and wings were bound tightly. It was not afraid, it simply surveyed me with its unflinching eye. I let it go and it flew off in the direction of the afternoon sun. It is not the first time, I thought, that an eagle has been caught in a gin.

January 31st.

Rode the mule down to Gilgil. Very hot. White horses careering about near the water filled me with alarm. I was directed to the office and there I sat for half an hour while an unpleasant pale-faced accountant catechised R. I looked at his hard conceited face and yellow gaiters and hated him.

February 12th.

Worked all day. In the evening a boy came for Posho. I went across with Masharia to give him some. The Pleiades were far up above a cedar tree which had something of the shape of a Tintinhull elm. "I have often seen those seven stars in England." "What are the stars?" I asked him. "Moto Mungu. "Eyes of God," he rapped out without a moment's hesitation.

Once more I got an odd sensation as though perhaps there really was a capricious negroid diety up there, around, everywhere.

March 2d.

Weighed barley and whitewashed pigsty. Read a report of the funeral of the Countess Poulett at Hinton St. George. How pitiful are all our efforts to conceal, to cast a veil over the ghastly reality within the coffin. God! I have seen dead faces. I know what they look like. I know what they say.

March 13th.

Unloaded barley straw. Often throughout the day my mind reverted to scenes and sensations at home. What about the first early days of Spring? The feel and the smell of the first sunny days? What about the clear early evening light and dry March dust in Bere High Street as I saw it that afternoon two years ago?

Here in Africa the sun and the black men and the vast tracts of land make all different and also there are no daffodils here, no meadow sweet and no wood anemones.